Gayatri Carole Rocherolle

The Landscape Diaries
Garden of Obsession

RUDER FINN PRESS
301 East 57th Street New York, NY 10022

Editor~
Lavanya Ghose Muller

Photography~
Richard Felber, Darlyne Murawski
Gayatri Carole Rocherolle

Illustrations~
Edward Henrey, Gretchen Kyle

Designer~
Lavanya Ghose Muller

Productions~
Shanti Bithi Books
www.shantibithi.com

Artistic consultant~
Caroline M. Rocherolle

Dedicated to
Sri Chinmoy
with infinite gratitude

Photo Credits

© **2003 Richard Felber:** front & back covers, pages 108-109, 114
© **2006 Richard Felber:** pages i   xi, 31, 50 56, 58, 60, 61, 70, 73, 75–79, 81, 84, 87–122, 124, 126, 130, 134, 144–146, 164, 167–168, 173
www.richardfelberphotography.com

© **2006 Darlyne Murawski:** pages 64–69, 169–171
www.darlynemurawski.com

© **2006 Gayatri C. Rocherolle:** pages 4, 8, 35, 38–40, 52–54, 57, 63, 72, 74, 80, 82, 83, 85, 86, 123, 125–129, 132, 133, 135, 136, 140–142, 152, 153, 158–159, 166
www.shantibithi.com

Unattributed photos are from the Rocherolle Family albums

Illustrations

© **2006 Edward Henrey:** pages 1, 11, 16, 25, 27, 33, 41, 43, 45, 47, 59, 71, 131, 137, 147, 150—151
www.edwardhenrey.com

© **2006 Gretchen Kyle:** pages xv, 5, 15, 20, 42, 48, 60, 126, 128, 162, 163, 172
www.shadesofgre.com

© **2006 Papaha Jeff Gosline:** page iii
www.papaha.com

© **2006 Serge Bachelier:** page 133

© **Christie's Images Ltd., 1992:** Renoir oil, page xvii

© **2006 Artists Rights Society (ARS)**, New York/ADAGP, Paris: Vuillard pastel, page xii

Courtesy of Sotheby's: Vuillard pastel, page xii; Renoir oil, page 7

Copyright © 2006 Gayatri Carole Rocherolle

Copyright © 2006 Ruder Finn Press

Second edition, first printing 2007

Library of Congress Control Number: 2006926665

ISBN 10: 1-932646-38-8
ISBN 13: 978-1-932646-38-2

Facing page: *Primula japonica* 'Redfield Strain'

Grateful Acknowledgment

To Judy and Michael Steinhardt

for their encouragement,
kindness,
generosity of spirit,
and for
their passionate commitment
to their garden

Magnolia 'Elizabeth,' gift of the Brooklyn Botanic Garden

TABLE OF CONTENTS

Betula nigra 'Heritage'

Betula jacquemontii

Edouard Vuillard
"Lady with a Veil"
(1902) pastel on brown paper

PROLOGUE

When I ran away in 1965 at the age of 20, I packed eight giant suitcases and withdrew all of my money (about $3,000) from the East New York Savings Bank. I used almost a third of my savings to purchase a one-way First Class ticket on the final voyage of the Queen Mary.

My boyfriend, Jerome, was to give notice to his boss at Firmenich, a Swiss fragrance company, as soon as I left, and join me in London by Christmas at the latest. Although we had no idea where we would live when he arrived, or how we would find work, none of that seemed to matter; we were young and in love. Our parents had mounted a campaign to prevent us from marrying. My departure on the Queen Mary was the best we could come up with in the face of their disapproval.

I had the use of my family's 1958 Cadillac convertible to drive to and from college in Boston. "The blue canoe," as my college roommate Boge referred to it, had a huge trunk. I drove this oversized car home on the two weekends before my departure to secretly pack and haul away as many of my belongings as I could. My parents never noticed anything unusual when I affectionately bid them farewell. They assumed I was returning to Tufts.

Before taking a taxi to the pier, I parked their car in the garage of the Regency Hotel where they kept an apartment. Worried about the parking charges that would accrue, I mailed the parking stub along with the letter that would inform them of my whereabouts.

My older sister, Roz, was aware of my plans because I had entrusted her with some of my precious savings, which she was to wire to me in London when I needed it. She insisted on coming to the boat to see me off, but mainly to persuade me to change my mind. I was as headstrong then as I am now. I not only ignored her pleas, but also swore her to secrecy. Roz was forbidden to tell my parents anything until she knew they had received my letter. She tearfully disembarked at the final call, and with the loud horn blasting, just like in the movies, the ship set sail into the cold morning fog.

It was an early November crossing, and the sea was so rough that grip ropes were put up on the decks. I was one of only four passengers who made it to the dining room for all the meals. Most of the others were too queasy to leave their cabins. In First Class they served caviar for breakfast, lunch, and dinner. My appetite did not desert me. I made sure to have the caviar even for breakfast, and was grateful that in this case I had listened to my sister, who had advised me to begin taking Dramamine even before the boat sailed.

Roz took the fall for my disappearance. My unsuspecting parents, thinking I was still at school, were distraught when they received my letter, and furious that my sister had kept her word to me by not telling them what I was about to do. My mother arranged to fly to London at once, and purchased a ticket for Jerome, whom she "invited" to accompany her. She hoped to escort me back to New York immediately, but I insisted on two days of shopping in London before capitulating.

My father had wanted to be the one who brought me home, but his doctor warned him that the trip would be too stressful for his heart. I will never forget the disappointment in his voice when he reached me by phone onboard the ship. "Your mother is coming, sweetheart, but you know if I were able to come, it would be me."

Only one year before this, my sister and I had accompanied him to London to attend the fall art auctions at Sotheby's. On that trip my dad had done something really sweet. Unbeknownst to me, he had sent a ticket to my best friend Mona, who was at school in Grenoble, France, so she could join us for the week. She surprised me and Roz when she called us from the lobby of our London hotel shortly after we checked in.

Looking back, I realize that I never understood the privileges I had growing up: the use of our box at the Ballet and the Opera, season tickets to the Philharmonic at Lincoln Center, and 5th row center seats for all the great Broadway productions. On the wall of my bedroom at 188 Kings Point Road on Long Island hung a Renoir oil painting of a woman playing a guitar (page xvii), a Chagall wedding scene, and two Robert Henri portraits.

If I had any conscious sense of what it meant to live in a home with these immortal canvases, I cannot remember. My brother, Jon, used to annoyingly throw a soccer ball at the wall between a giant Lautrec oil

Photographed on board RMS QUEEN MARY.

On deck as the ship set sail (I'm in the light trench coat at far left)

My dad, Lester Avnet, greets an ambassador in his art-filled office

for others as well as for our family. His childlike and loving heart had endeared him to many. When my dad went to the other world, we received telegrams and letters of condolence from the president, vice-president, senators and judges, in addition to our close friends and family members.

My father didn't want his children to be burdened with the responsibility of great wealth. He wanted us to have our own goals, and the satisfaction of working to fulfil them. Upon his death, my parents' collection of 19th and 20th Century drawings went to the Museum of Modern Art—the largest drawing bequest to MOMA of that time. In his will he did not forget any of the 19 other charities and trusts that he had supported during his lifetime.

Lester Avnet was a divine warrior who fought against racial and religious intolerance. His boundless enthusiasm, and his faith in our capacity to succeed at whatever we tried, were tremendous boons for my brother, my sister, and me. It has taken many years for me to fully comprehend the profound and loving influence he had on my life.

painting and a Vuillard pastel (page xii). A Monet watercolor was out of reach for him: it hung over our parents' bed. We owned more than thirteen hundred works of art. When we ran out of space to hang paintings and drawings in our home, my dad had the windows of his corner office in the Time & Life Building boarded up so he could have a floor-to-ceiling display of the drawings that he so loved (photo above).

Life in the 1960's was full of exciting events. Dad's company, Avnet, Inc., was the high flier of the day, and its stock was on the "most active" list for weeks on end. With all my father's fundraising and humanitarian activities, his world brought me into contact with many distinguished and remarkable people: Martin Luther King, Jr., Sidney Poitier, and many U.N. am-bassadors and dignitaries. I took the goodness of my life in stride, as teenagers do, and didn't feel different from my friends.

It was not until Daddy passed away in 1970, and I heard his death reported every hour on 1010 WINS News, that I realized how significant and meaningful his life had been

My parents at the opening of an exhibit of their Old Master drawing collection in West Palm Beach, Florida, 1969.
This traveling exhibit, which circulated the country for two years, was sponsored by the American Federation of Arts.
Jean-Honoré Fragonard: *Susannah and the Elders* (far left)
Jean-Baptiste Greuze: *The Father's Curse—The Ungrateful Son* (center)
Jean Antoine Watteau: *Two Studies of a Seated Woman* (far right)

Pierre-Auguste Renoir
"Femme à la guitare"
(1897) oil on canvas
This painting hung in my Kings Point bedroom.

Overleaf: Cutting the cake on my 22nd birthday

CHAPTER 1
THE HONEYMOON IS OVER

Jerome and I gave my parents one month to plan our wedding, because we wanted it small and we didn't want too much fussing over the details. My mother still managed to plan a beautiful and romantic country wedding for 225 guests at our home on the water in Kings Point. And to satisfy my father, we had a reception for 200 of his business friends the previous week. The pre-wedding was an exact replica of the wedding—tent, music and all.

Because I was attending summer school at the time, Jerome and I decided to take our wedding trip after I finished my classes two weeks later. We were going to spend a month in France so that there would be enough time for me to meet all of my new relatives.

First we spent a week in Corsica, arriving at one o'clock in the morning with no hotel reservations during the height of the summer season. But this turned out not to be a serious matter, as we managed to persuade the front desk at a very nice hotel on the water to give us their last available room because we were honeymooners.

However, here is where I should have paid more attention. We were dining one evening in the hotel's outdoor restaurant overlooking the Mediterranean. It was a beautiful clear night, and our food had been served. We heard a buzzing sound that gradually grew louder and louder. I actually ignored it, but Jerome, who was sitting opposite me, saw that the noise was coming from an airplane that was flying quite low toward the terrace. As the noise increased, he became so alarmed that he jumped up, knocking over his chair, and ran off the terrace and into the hotel. Apparently, he was convinced that the plane was about to crash into the terrace where we were sitting.

But this is the part that surprised me: He did not say anything to me about the airplane, which I could not see because my back was to it. When he ran for cover, he never bothered to mention to me that I might want to come with him out of the path of this incoming plane. In fact, he just got up and ran, without saying a word.

Poor Jerome! All the other diners knew that this was the mail plane that buzzed the hotel every other night. No one else budged from their seat or stopped enjoying their dinner even for a moment on that beautiful moonlit evening. Jerome had to nonchalantly return to the table, pick up his chair, and resume his interrupted meal.

I was puzzled that he had neglected to mention to his new bride that

we both appeared to be in harm's way. But his having to return to the restaurant totally embarrassed was satisfying enough, so I just teased him about it for many days. He took my ribbing good-naturedly.

From Corsica we went on to France, and I met Bonne Maman, my father-in-law's 92-year-old mother, at La Rocherolle, the family chateau. At

Château de la Rocherolle, près de Tendu

that time, she had a secretary, Madame Fraval, and three other servants. But Jerome showed me the seven bells that she still kept near her, which, during her earlier years, were used for calling her attendants. A different sound summoned each person.

I was a little taken aback. The castle was poorly lit, damp, and felt creepy to me. I did not fall in love with it. And Bonne Maman had a strange

habit of not speaking directly to me. She would address Jerome in French, saying, "*Elle est très drôle, ta femme,*" (Your wife is very odd) or, "*Pourquoi est-ce qu'elle ne mange pas?*" (Why isn't she eating?). Well, it is true that I wasn't eating, and that was because it made me queasy to watch her consume ten carefully prepared *boules* (round patties) of raw horsemeat, which the doctor had prescribed for her anemia.

Jerome really wanted me to have a nice experience, as this was my first meeting with his relatives in France. It didn't seem to be going too well at the castle. But meeting his sister Marie-Laure and her husband, Michel, was quite a different matter. Jerome had promised that I would love them, and I did. I was introduced to assorted aunts, uncles, and cousins along the way, my French was improving, and the best part was yet to come.

We had arranged to meet my friend, Mona Riklis (now Ackerman), and her husband of six months, Irwin, in Paris. Who would not want their best friend on their honeymoon? Mona and I shopped in Paris together, our dream come true, and then we all drove to

wood-paneled upstairs bedrooms, each with a view of the Atlantic Ocean, were off-limits for us.

After two weeks with Mona and Irwin, our honeymoon trip was coming to an end. The four of us went to the airport together to take our TWA flight back to New York. I boarded the plane ahead of Jerome, anxious to settle into my seat because I was carrying aboard

the stewardess over and told her my husband was not on board. She paged him right away, and he was located. Jerome, my husband of six weeks, was sitting in First Class!

The stewardess asked him if he would like to move back to Economy Class so that we could sit together. He refused, saying there was no way he was going back to the crowded part of the plane. They had offered him a First Class seat as he was boarding, and he had taken it. Why would he consider giving up this great seat?

I was upset that I would not be sitting next to my new husband, but I tried not to show it. Fighting back tears, I told the stewardess we were on our honeymoon. She took pity on me and arranged to move me into First Class with Jerome. He joked about it, saying he knew all along that they would put me in First Class if he would not move back to Economy.

I don't really believe that he was thinking about that when he agreed to accept the upgrade. What I was beginning to realize was that it was going to be every man for himself. And I wasn't wrong.

Park-ar-Lann, Perros-Guirec, Bretagne

Park-ar-Lann, the family beach house in Perros-Guirec, Brittany. This house was so large that the German officers had set up their local headquarters in it during WWII.

Despite the fact that Bonne Maman had not been to Perros in more than seven years, the elderly caretaker, Jeanne, insisted that we sleep in rooms on the lower level. She informed us in no uncertain terms that the beautiful

a large and heavy crystal vase that had been a wedding gift from Marie-Laure and Michel. Mona and Irwin were snuggled up together in the row behind me, but Jerome was nowhere in sight.

As I waited in my seat, the plane began to fill up. Still there was no sign of Jerome. When it looked like they were about to close the airplane doors, I became alarmed. I called

Halesia monticola 'Rosea'—a gift of the Brooklyn Botanic Garden

CHAPTER 2
MY PROMISE

Before I married Jerome, my one and only job, other than working for my father, was working for my best friend Mona's father, Meshulam Riklis, at his office in New York City. My mother was quite happy that I was working in New York, because it meant that I could stay with my dad at our apartment in the Regency Hotel during the week.

On Friday evenings Perry, our chauffeur, would drive Daddy and me back home to Kings Point, Long Island, in our navy blue limousine. On the way, my father would often hand me a stack of crumpled newspaper clippings about his company that he had stashed in his jacket pocket.

One particular evening he was in a pensive mood. He asked me to move over in the back seat and sit closer to him. I did, and he recited a poem by Edna St. Vincent Millay, which he told me was his favorite. It began:

> My candle burns at both ends,
> It will not last the night.
> But ah, my foes,
>   and oh, my friends
> It gives a lovely light.

He explained that he would not be around forever, and that he wanted me to make him a promise. I immediately agreed, without even knowing what he would ask. He went on, "You will take care of your mother. The others will not do this. But you will do this for me; you will do this."

"I promise you, Daddy. Of course I will."

Many years later, I did exactly what my father had asked me to do. For three and a half years, when my mother was suffering from Alzheimer's, I was the one, of her three children, who took responsibility for her care.

One summer afternoon, actually on my 49th birthday, I drove into New York City to visit my mother at her apartment on Fifth Avenue. I found a parking space right in front of her building, and felt very lucky. But I was feeling something more, as

Troy Avenue, Brooklyn, August 1945

a sudden rush of tears made me fumble for my purse. I *was* lucky, I told myself, and it was because my father had asked me to make a promise so many years ago, and I was now keeping that promise.

During the years that I faithfully looked after my mother, I felt that I was once again working for my father, fulfilling the promise I had made to him. By then it was almost twenty-five years after his death, and I was still working for him. That thought made taking care of my mother a little easier. But still, it was not easy.

I remember so clearly the day I realized that something was terribly wrong with her. I was coming down the staircase of my sister's house in Washington, D.C. Mommy had flown up from Palm Beach, where she spent winters, to attend my nephew Ben's *Bar Mitzvah*. She was standing at the bottom of the stairs, looking at me as I came down, and for a moment it seemed as though she didn't recognize me. I was only five feet away from her, but she was looking at me as if I were a complete stranger. I froze on the stairs, afraid to take the next step, which would confirm my suspicions. At that moment my mother did not know who I was.

Less than a year after that day, my brother Jon, sister Roz, and I took our mother for a visit to the Hebrew Home for the Aged in Riverdale. Jon hired a limousine to take all of us there together. Mommy clung to Jon's arm and did not speak a word during the entire ride to the Bronx.

Was my mother going to spend her last days in the Bronx, I wondered. It was a place so unfamiliar to me. We had moved from Brooklyn to Long Island, and then to Manhattan. Why the Bronx? But we were taking her to see a place that was highly recommended for people with Alzheimer's. I had trouble swallowing the word as I sat silently in the car, watching my mother's fear rise up in her frail and strangely unkempt body.

After the interview with the medical staff, Mommy pulled my brother aside. "Let's get out of here, Jon," she said. He managed to smile at her newfound assertiveness and conviction. "This place is not for me. This is for sick people!" And that was that. It was her last important decision.

When the time came, we hired round-the-clock Irish nurses to care for Mommy in her own home. There were two on duty at all times during the day, and one for the night shift. Jon, who lived in Topanga, California, was so distraught by our mother's deterioration that he found it often too painful to visit with her. We all agreed that Roz, whose solace was shopping, would have the responsibility of buying our mother clothing so that she was always beautifully dressed. Roz visited to bring Mommy her new outfits, but she still lived and worked in Washington, D.C. Her visits were not as frequent as I would have liked.

It fell to me, the middle child, to manage the team of nurses that lovingly and devotedly made Mommy's life as comfortable and familiar as they could. I hired them, settled their disputes, re-hired them, encouraged them, adored them, gave them their paychecks, and visited as often as I could, never less than one or two days a week. This was how I was able to keep my mother as safe and comfortable as she could be, considering that she lived in her own home for three and a half years more, until the end stage of a disease that attempts to rob you of your very soul.

There were days when my mother pulled at my coat like a child when I walked toward the foyer. "Don't leave me!" she would shout as I closed her front door. And later on there were days when she never even noticed as I left her apartment to go back to my life in Connecticut as best I could.

We spared no expense for our mother's care. Sometimes the nursing costs approached $300,000 per year, but we wanted to give her the best that we could. I occasionally wondered what she would have thought about the extravagant cost of her care. Before she became ill, my mother was a person who turned lights off whenever she left a room, to save electricity. She even turned her fridge off when she went down to Palm Beach for the winter. But these were no longer her choices, and I know in her lucid moments she was all too aware of that.

One time, as I walked Mommy slowly around the living room, she paused in front of her only remaining Renoir painting, "*La Coiffure*" (right). "Now nothing is mine anymore," she whispered to me out of earshot of the nurses. It was true; her life was ours, and no one felt the burden of that more than I.

Pierre-Auguste Renoir:
"La Coiffure" (Gabrielle)
(1895) oil on canvas

Cercis canadensis 'Alba'

CHAPTER 3

OUR ESTEEMED COUNSEL

In December of 1969 I went down to Palm Peach with my 18-month-old son to visit my father, who was in the hospital. He was suffering from heart failure, and I could tell, by what my mother was not saying, that this was serious. One afternoon his doctor called me out into the corridor and said, "I told your father to put his house in order." I knew, but I didn't know, that the end was near. I was 24 years old.

I was afraid to tell my mother what the doctor had said, so I called her close friend Stella Fishbach and asked if I could come and see her. As soon as I arrived at Stella's apartment I burst into tears. "The doctor told me Daddy should put his house in order," I confided between sobs.

"Carole dear, does mother have her own lawyer?" Stella inquired.

I was startled by her question. "Daddy has a lawyer—his company lawyer," I replied. "But I don't actually know if Mommy has her own lawyer."

Stella suggested that we get in touch with her closest friend, Lillian Poses, and gave me a phone number where we could reach Lillian, who was vacationing in Barbados. There seemed to be a great urgency to her suggestion, so when I returned to our apartment I told Rozzie, who was on break from Harvard Law School at the time. She found Daddy's will, called Lillian Poses, whom we had never met or even heard of before that day, and read her the will over the telephone.

To summarize, Daddy had made the Chemical Bank one of the executors of his will, and he had recently

Lillian L. Poses

taken out a loan from that bank, secured by shares of stock in his own company, Avnet, Inc. When he had written his will, the company stock had been at 46. It had fallen since that time, along with all the semiconductor stocks, and apparently having that bank as executor could be disastrous for us. The bank had a conflict of interest, Lillian informed us. She dictated a codicil to Rozzie, and we presented it to our father in the hospital.

"Daddy, can you sign this?" I asked, trembling at the thought of what I would be witnessing. With his trademark smile, he signed the codicil to his will: With Love, Lester Avnet.

We were extremely grateful to Lillian for alerting us to this potential problem. My Dad passed away only days after we first spoke with her. Without her concern and wise counsel, my father's entire estate might have been bankrupt.

Lillian became our trusted family attorney from that day forward. It took her eleven years to settle my father's estate, as it included hundreds of works of art that had to be sold in order to raise capital. This was something that could not be done overnight. Lillian was forced to negotiate with every one of the nineteen charities that were mentioned in the will, each one insisting

that they be paid without delay. We were now dealing with hard-nosed professionals, she explained to us. These were not the same people who had courted our father for pledges and donations. One prominent university even sued the estate.

The world became a different place for Joan Avnet, wife of the late Lester Avnet. Friends—or supposed friends—deserted her when my father was no longer by her side. More than anyone else, our family depended on Lillian, who preserved my mother's dignity in an unfamiliar and indifferent world.

Lester Avnet (far left) honoring sculptor Sir Henry Moore (center) with Dr. Samuel Belkin, then president of Yeshiva University. My parents founded the Joan and Lester Avnet Institute of Molecular Biology. Upon my mother's death, Albert Einstein College of Medicine received the proceeds of a large trust that had been set up during my father's lifetime.

CHAPTER 4
THE NURSERY: PARTNER FOR A DAY

In the spring of 1970, Jerome and I moved out of Manhattan and into an adorable house in Stamford, Connecticut. Lexy, our baby, was almost two years old at the time, and we were expecting a second child in the fall. My husband did not want to commute into the city, so we built a tiny cottage at the edge of our property, that he could use as a perfume laboratory.

I was intrigued by the antique perfume bottles his father had given us from their family business, Roger & Gallet. I loved the scale with the weights, the bottles of essential oils, and all the perfume paraphernalia that was so unfamiliar to me. Jerome went right to work in our tiny laboratory, creating a rose-scented spray that florists might want to use on their cut roses. Over the years, horticulturists had hybridized roses to be showy, long-stemmed, and durable. Florists loved them, but the downside was that many of these roses no longer had any noticeable fragrance.

The spray that Jerome created was very pure, and it smelled exactly like an old-fashioned rose. We thought maybe we had something, and my mother loved it. In fact, she loved it so much that she bought almost our entire stock of *Jardin de Rose* for herself and her friends in Palm Beach. We were in and out of the rose spray business within a year. That was okay with me. My thinking then was: you try something, and if you're lucky enough to sell out, you get out while you're ahead.

But we still had a laboratory full of essential oils, so we tried something else: We designed a perfume kit for children, which we called Invent-a-Scent. It was a clever idea, but it took us so many months to get the styrofoam mold for our presentation that we missed the annual Toy Industry Trade Show.

We were full of ideas when we put our heads together, but ideas don't always translate into earning a living. I was starting to realize how much my life had changed since my father's death, and I began to feel anxious about what we were going to do next.

Then early one morning Jerome drove a U-Haul up to Holdridge Farm Nursery near his family beach house in Groton, Connecticut, and returned home with a truckload of bushes and flowers. Without telling me, he had rented the parking lot of the deli around the corner from our house. "We have six weeks to sell everything," he reassured me.

Jerome unloaded the trees while I arranged the flowers in colorful rows. We put rolls of yellow and white contact paper on the deli's dumpster, and in big black letters we spelled out: THE NURSERY. We were in business.

We decided that I would do the selling and he would stay home, just around the corner, with our 3-year-old and 11-month-old boys. I wished he would have come up to help more often. When a customer looked as if they were going to wander into the parking lot and look over our flowers, I was terrified. I would sometimes hide in the back seat of the car just to avoid having to answer questions. I didn't know anything about plants.

A young boy, clumsy and not too bright, was working in the deli at the time. He took pity on me and used to come out and keep me company. That became the routine. Richie would come out to encourage me, and pretty soon he was the one who was collecting the money. He even brought me a grey cash box and convinced me to get a folding table to set it on.

Richie was 14, overweight and slovenly, but he was my new friend, and he was always happy to help out. He loved counting money, he was not shy, and he had a talent for selling. I now had my first worker and, unbeknownst to me, "partner for a day," as my accountant explained to me years later.

We had an illustrious group of customers at THE NURSERY: Alice and Benny Goodman, Arthur 'Punch' Sulzberger of *The New York Times*, Jack Paar, and many others who lived in the area. At the end of our fourth week of business, Herb Oscar Anderson, a popular disk jockey at the time, drove into the parking lot in a big black car. He sauntered through the remaining rows of bushes, then came up to me and said, "I'll take it."

"Which ones would you like?" I asked.

"I said I'll take it," he repeated.

"Excuse me, I don't understand," I stammered.

"I'll take the rest of whatever is here. Everything. And I'll be back in an hour to pick it up."

So two weeks early, we closed THE NURSERY, our first enterprise. We had $3,000 in our pocket, and we were once again unemployed.

CHAPTER 5
THE 20-YEAR LEASE

Mrs. Jones owned the deli whose parking lot we had rented for The Nursery, and an historic house next door to it. (It is reputed that George Washington may have slept there.) She was well into her eighties at the time that we became interested in the house next door to the deli.

We had heard that Mrs. Jones was a difficult person to deal with and, more importantly, that her daughters were downright unpleasant. After the success we had had in the parking lot of the deli, Jerome was determined to rent the little house so that we could open a real plant nursery.

By a stroke of good luck, old Mrs. Jones hated the man now leasing the store on the corner because he had turned it into a deli; it was no longer a quaint country store, as it had been when her husband was alive.

Jerome courted Mrs. Jones and commiserated with her about the demise of her late husband's country store. Her daughters were like guard dogs, so he would try to see her when they were not around. This went on for months, until finally he asked her to let him rent the tiny house and land at 3047 High Ridge Road. Mostly to spite the deli owner, who had been trying to rent it for years, Mrs. Jones agreed. She obviously intended to continue hating him from the next world, because when we presented her with a 20-year lease for $200 per month, increasing by only 5% every five years, old Mrs. Jones signed it without hesitating.

It was an exciting time for us; we finally had a permanent place

Ready to open!

Lillian did more for us than write our 20-year lease. During our bi-monthly visits with her, she taught us invaluable lessons the old-fashioned way—with stories told over and over again.

Her favorite and most often-repeated lesson to us, as a young couple, was: "We, not I." Whenever I excitedly told her about something I had done at our nursery, now named Friendship Farm and Nursery, she would say, "No dear—we, not I." And the same was true for Jerome. If he began, "Lillian, I did such and such for a client," she would interrupt him, "No Jerome—we, not I. The two of you together are always better than one."

to set up shop. When we were almost ready to open for business, one little problem remained to be solved. The building inspector paid us an unannounced visit one day and intimated that we might not be able to open after all. We were dumbfounded.

When anything went wrong in our life, there was always one person we turned to for advice: Lillian Poses, now my mother's trusted friend, as well as our family attorney. Lillian had been the first woman to graduate from New York University Law School – and at such a young age that she had had to wait a year before being admitted to the bar in New York.

Our esteemed counsel must have made a phone call on our behalf, because two days later the building inspector returned, and his attitude had remarkably changed.

CHAPTER 6

MEDITATION

Less than a year after my father passed away, Jerome read an article in the Sunday *New York Times,* entitled "Yoga Comes to Connecticut." For several months, he had been practicing yoga with an instructor in New York City. The idea that a yoga teacher would be available in Connecticut, and he would no longer have to drive into the city for classes, was very appealing.

The following evening, thinking he was going to an exercise class, Jerome went to see the yoga teacher, Sri Chinmoy, in Wilton. "It wasn't an exercise class," he told me when he returned home that night. "But whatever it was, I liked it."

For the next few weeks, every Monday evening Jerome would leave for yoga meditation in Wilton. But he was always so cheerful and lighthearted in anticipation of his Monday night out that I began to think maybe he had a girlfriend. One Monday evening, right before he was about to leave, I dressed hurriedly and said, "I arranged for a babysitter. I'm coming with you."

What I experienced that night was entirely unexpected. During the one-hour silent meditation, when I looked at the Guru, I saw my father sitting there instead. It was almost too much for me, because I didn't believe in those kinds of things. My mind was telling me this was not real, but my heart was flooded with peace. The silence was deep and profoundly comforting.

At the time, I was a nursing mother, and I didn't like leaving my boys for any reason. It was several months before I attended meditation again, and it was years before I understood how important meditation is for my inner peace and happiness.

Sri Chinmoy, or "Guru" (teacher) as we affectionately call him, has been a source of tremendous inspiration for my entire family. We have made the practice of meditation a part of our daily life. It has strengthened us in ways I could never have imagined.

Within a few years, each of us received a spiritual name from Guru: Narendra, Durdam, Gayatri, and Gangadhar. These names evoke our soul's predominant qualities.

Narendra (our older son) means "king among men, captain among men, supreme among men."

Our younger son's spiritual name is Durdam — "indomitable divine warrior."

My name is Gayatri, "the Goddess of Creativity, whose light and love permeates all the planes of consciousness."

And Jerome is now Gangadhar, "the source of the Ganges," and "one who purifies and nourishes the earth-plane."

Although my husband and I do not use these names professionally, we are called Gangadhar and Gayatri by our family and friends. I will use these names in my stories from now onward, though I may occasionally refer to us as Jerome and Carole.

Our family with Sri Chinmoy after a Masters Track Meet in Long Beach, California, 1987

CHAPTER 7
FRIENDSHIP FARM

In 1971 Gangadhar's father arranged for Pierre Marandon, a young Frenchman from Argenton-sur-Creuse, the town neighboring La Rocherolle, to be our intern. Pierre's father owned a recycling business, and it was understood that Pierre would take over the family business in time. This was to be an opportunity for him to learn American business ways and, his father hoped, how to speak English.

When Pierre arrived at Friendship Farm, we had boxes and boxes of cookware, garden supplies, and other goodies that had not yet been unpacked. In fact, the store had not even opened for business. Pierre was a little surprised that he had come to such a young enterprise, but were we ever fortunate to have him!

Pierre did not speak a word of English when he arrived. Standing 6 feet 5 inches tall, he probably found his living quarters in the tiny attic room above the store cramped, but he never complained. He cleverly devised a pull-down counter over the free-standing bathtub, to serve as his kitchen for light cooking, but he ate most of his meals with us. With Pierre's help, we opened Friendship Farm and Nursery.

No wonder we ultimately succeeded in our enterprise. Pierre was a brilliant, dynamic, and confident worker who set a standard that we always tried to live up to, even long after he was gone. Having the experience and confidence that we so sorely lacked, he taught us a lot about business, and especially about

Baby Durdam on opening day, with Narendra hiding in the doorway.

the bottom line. *"Le bénéfice— il faut dix pour cent"* was one of his favorite sayings. (You have to make at least a 10% profit.) Pierre loved doing business, and would often brag, *"J'ai fait une affaire aujourd'hui."* (I did some real business today.)

As his English improved, Pierre also became our trucker. He had been the trucker for *Marandon et Fils*, logging hundreds of kilometers on dangerous French roads, so picking up local nursery stock was child's play to Pierre. He had an active social life as well, and got to know many of the young women in the neighborhood. Often he would be out all night, but he would show up for work promptly at starting time (7 A.M.), and never tell us until the end of the day that he had not slept even one hour the night before.

Pierre knew absolutely nothing about trees, shrubs and flowers. But he had so much self-confidence,

Pierre standing in the front yard of Friendship Farm

and we were so busy running the nursery, that we sent him out to do our very first planting job. It was for a Mr. J on Lost District Drive in New Canaan, only two miles from our nursery. Pierre still occasionally asks us how his plantings look. They look horrible, to tell the truth, but we quickly learned to do better ourselves.

From Pierre's bold foray into planting, other requests followed, and in the course of that year we gradually became landscapers. Once Gangadhar saw that he could work outside the nursery, his design wheels started to turn. I was left to unload deliveries, water and tend the endless rows of flowers and bushes, and serve customers at the store. Some days my only helpers were our two little boys.

One day Mr. N, who was president of a huge conglomerate, hired us to landscape the backyard of his "McMansion," also in the Lost District area. I went to see the property on the afternoon the work was completed. Mr. N was praising my husband to the skies. He told Gangadhar what a beautiful job he had done, how he had transformed the yard (he truly had!), and how talented Gangadhar was (he was!).

When we returned to the store that afternoon, we did something we had never done before. Since Gangadhar had gone to the job every day to design the garden and supervise his workers (a practice he continues to this day), we decided to charge Mr. N for Gangadhar's time. We included in the bill a modest fee for design and supervision.

When I say Mr. N was enraged at this extra charge, I am not exaggerating. He telephoned Friendship Farm, demanding an explanation for the $60 design/supervision fee, and he flatly refused to pay it. This was a small disappointment, but Gangadhar was hooked on the feeling that he could transform an unremarkable house by making the property into something special.

CHAPTER 8

THE FRENCH CONNECTION

If my father had been alive, he probably would have helped us to buy the property we were renting for our nursery. But life was different for me now. My French in-laws were wonderful people, but not like Jewish relatives. For one thing, they never asked any personal questions. They never asked if things were going all right or if, for instance, we needed money. In fact, there was no important subject that was ever directly broached. Things were hinted at.

One thing they hinted at was that it would be nice for Gangadhar's father Guy ("Bon Pappy") to have something to occupy his time upon his retirement as President of Roger & Gallet. He was expected to retire within the next few months. Gangadhar's parents planned to spend six months of each year in France and six months in the U.S.

We had just built a large greenhouse, and our nursery was becoming popular. The greenhouse was filled with houseplants, which were in vogue at the time. Bon Pappy was an amateur horticulturist. His childhood home in Versailles had had acres of formal gardens, and he still had his own greenhouses full of flowers. So Guy Rocherolle became Friendship Farm's resident expert six months of the year. The customers loved him—a charming man with a heavy French accent. How lucky we were to have someone with his business and horticultural skills working for free!

Guy and Monique's engagement photo in the family greenhouse at Versailles, 1931

Gangadhar's mother's side of the family was artistic and independent-minded, according to my husband. As the story goes, her grandfather Gustave Lyon, known as Panos, wanted to inherit the family piano business. After a fierce struggle with his two brothers-in-law, André and Edouard Michelin, Panos finally won. *Maison Pleyel* was his, and the two Michelin brothers were left money. With their inheritance they started a small tire company . . .

Panos was an inventor, a designer, and an acoustical genius. In additon to running *Maison Pleyel*,

he designed and built *la salle Pleyel*, France's equivalent of Carnegie Hall. The opening of *la salle Pleyel* in October, 1927 was attended by the President of the Republic, ministers, ambassadors, countesses, duchesses, princesses, and even a maharajah. The famed architect Le Corbusier attended the opening as well. He and Panos had collaborated on other design projects. Le Corbusier was so impressed with the design of the *salle Pleyel* that he wrote a beautiful letter of congratulation to his friend.

Monique Lyon ("Granny") adored her grandfather Panos. During her childhood, great musicians were part of the extended family. Stravinsky spent almost five years in a studio at *la salle Pleyel*. Pablo Casals was another frequent guest, as were Robert Casadesus, Ravel, and Grieg. Granny's family apartment was in the same building as the concert hall, and it had a tiny sliding aperture through which she could view and listen to all the performances of these musical immortals.

Gangadhar's parents visited the garden that is the main focus of this book during the early years, when we were frantically building and planting. But his father did not live to see the completion of our project. He passed away in 1994 at the age of 88. I could see how amazed he was with the scope of the gardens, but

he said little. I suppose he thought, "*Il est un peu comme son arrière grand-père.*" (He is a bit like his great grandfather.)

My father-in-law was convinced that all blossoming talents, as well as unfortunate weaknesses, came from some ancestor, and he loved to pull out the portraits, with their uncanny resemblances to this one and that one, to prove it. Gangadhar always tells me that he prefers his mother's side of the family, the Lyons and Wolffs, because they are free-spirited creative souls, not like the Rocherolles and Roycourts, a more formal and stuffy group.

CHAPTER 9
LA ROCHEROLLE

Our boys in the courtyard of the castle during the summer of 1972

In 1972 Pierre Marandon returned to the United States for a summer holiday. Even though he protested that he was not coming back to work, he agreed to run Friendship Farm for several weeks so that we could take our first trip to La Rocherolle with the boys. This was a short visit, but it marked the beginning of our exposure to French horticulture.

While we were in France, we went to all the local nurseries to get ideas for Friendship Farm. Gangadhar took hundreds of out-of-focus pictures of me standing with this plant or that (photo left). Visiting nurseries, locating plants, and taking photos is a practice we continue to this day. I am now the designated photographer, and he is the one who stands smiling for the camera.

On that first family trip Bon Pappy took us to Gargilesse, a tiny village that was the summer home of Georges Sand, Chopin's mistress. Gargilesse is an historic artisan village, with tiny shops and a spectacular view of the beautiful *Vallée de la Creuse*. When we stopped in the shop of a young ironworker, Serge Bachelier, both of us were taken with this shy, talented artist. I convinced Gangadhar to let me purchase some of Serge's candlesticks for our own store, and chose two sets of heart candlesticks, one pair of tulips, three figures of cats, and two roosters. We were now importers of French art. The relationship we began with Serge Bachelier in 1972 will take us almost to the end of our landscape diaries, when a gate we commissioned from him 31 years later was ultimately featured in *Architectural Digest*.

The visit to Gargilesse was the only thing we did that summer, other than eat enormous meals and swim in *le lavoir*, a freezing cold spring-fed basin of water adjacent to the *potager*, the castle's large walled vegetable and flower garden. Our *potager*, with its endless rows of delphinium, daisies, roses, and dahlias, was so floriferous that the Comtesse Jean le Bault de la Morinière would come regularly to cut flowers for Le Prunjet, her chateau across the *Vallée de la Bouzanne*. My boys and their cousins affectionately referred to *la comtesse* as *"Madame Piscine,"* because they had a standing invitation to swim in her heated pool.

We had more flowers for cutting than I had ever seen in a private home. The garden was tended by Raoul, who had lived and worked at La Rocherolle for more than 40 years. He and his wife, Madeleine, served Bonne Maman until her death, and remained with Granny and Bon Pappy for many years afterwards. Raoul was a tyrant. Nobody dared pick vegetables or fruit in the *potager* without first getting his permission.

In 1974 we returned for a six-week visit to La Rocherolle. That summer all the cousins, one by one beginning with my boys, came down with *la varicelle* (chicken pox). Durdam, my four-year-old, had a terrible case. To make sure he didn't scratch and scar himself, I barely left his side for days.

I had brought only one book with me that summer, and I read it over and over as I sat in a chair next to my son's bed. It was Sri Chinmoy's *Commentary on The Bhagavad Gita*—a strange companion for a visit to the castle, but it's mantric prose was unexpectedly soothing.

When Durdam's condition improved, and he was finally able to sleep peacefully, I would venture into the tower next to his second-floor bedroom. From the window I could see for miles. It was a timeless view. Summers are hot and dry in

Serge in front of his atelier in Gargilesse, 1972

Le potager in bloom

this part of France. The fields were parched, but the sight of cows grazing along the Bouzanne River transported me.

So many people, over the past 500 years, had enjoyed this same view, and I wondered who they were and what their lives had been like.

Who had slept in the room I now laid claim to? It was intriguing to be part of the life and lore of a castle, especially this castle that bore our name.

Vue de la Vallée de Tende prise de Bourdesoulle (Indre).

Aerial view of *Château de la Rocherolle*

CHAPTER 10
ORGANIC APPLES

My husband loves organic apples. Everyone who knows him has seen him at some time with a small knife in his hand, peeling an apple. But he has a history with apples that goes far beyond clean healthy living.

In the 1970s we were looking for things to sell at our country store. In addition to the plant nursery, which was expanding, we had begun selling the finest Cordon Bleu cookware, beautiful copper pots, and anything French or for cooking. The natural progression from being one of the original complete cookware stores was to sell food. We were not licensed to sell food, but country stores could sell produce outdoors. Having a small farmer's market with local produce was something we began to consider.

One day my husband came up with one of his brilliant ideas. Gangadhar decided that he was going to become a distributor of organic apples—Filsinger apples, to be precise. They were grown in Canada, just north of Buffalo, and were known to be the purest, best-tasting apples you could find. I wasn't convinced that this was such a good idea, but there was no stopping him.

My friend Susie Miller's husband, Butch, whose family owned Queensboro Dairy, had been kind enough to sell us a giant white milk delivery truck for only $500. It was an old truck, but we made good use of it hauling nursery stock. Gangadhar decided he would use the old milk truck to pick up the apples.

He persuaded me to drive up to Vermont with my college roommate Suzy Fanger Marcus and her husband, Norman. "We can sell most of the apples at the organic food fair over the weekend, and whatever is left we'll keep for ourselves," he reassured me.

"I'll meet you there Saturday morning," he continued with a big grin. "Don't worry. It's the number one food fair in New England. And I'm only picking up a few dozen boxes of apples; people will love them."

Whenever my husband tells me not to worry, that is the moment I should begin to wonder what he is not telling me.

Gangadhar set out for Canada on a Thursday morning in our giant white milk truck. I arrived in Vermont with Suzy, Norman, and our two little boys late Friday night. Gangadhar did not arrive with the apples on Saturday morning, as he had promised. Early Saturday morning I received a telephone call from him, in which he said in a hushed voice: "I'll tell you later, but I won't be there till Sunday morning. We'll still have one day to sell. The apples are delicious." Click.

I spent the day walking around the food fair with my boys, too embarrassed to stand behind our empty table. As I watched the crowds of people stocking up on organic products, I became more and more disappointed and certain that my husband

had gotten himself into some kind of trouble.

By the time he arrived in Vermont with just under 200 cases of apples, it was late Sunday morning. The food fair was already winding down, and many vendors were packing up. We still managed to sell 40 boxes out of the back of our truck before we had to leave, but that left us with 153 forty-pound boxes of Filsinger apples.

Gangadhar had given away six boxes to an angry homeowner in whose driveway he had gotten stuck after getting lost, and one box to a policeman who had stopped the truck and found that he had no registration or driver's license on him. The passport my husband presented to the officer did not satisfy him, but fortunately the box of Filsinger apples did.

We were also minus ten hemlock trees, which Gangadhar had not noticed were in the truck when he departed from Stamford. Canadian customs would not allow him to bring trees into the country, so he had left them on the side of the road with the intention of picking them up again on his way home. Needless to say, they were nowhere to be found when he returned to the spot.

I was furious! Gangadhar had bought more than twice as many boxes as he had said he would, and now, what were we supposed to do with 153 boxes of organic apples that needed to be kept in cold storage?

Outhouse Orchards in North Salem, NY saved us. They agreed to store the apples for as long as we needed, free of charge. I was determined to sell every box of Filsinger apples after this fiasco.

In those days, there were only three health food stores in New York City that sold fresh produce. One was on the Upper East Side, one was on the West Side, and a third tiny store was way downtown. I got on the telephone and poured my heart out to these three struggling enterprises. Each store agreed to buy four boxes of apples from me, and more after that, if they sold well.

So each week, with proud defiance, I drove up to Outhouse Orchards, loaded my car with cases of apples, and then drove into the city to personally deliver them to the health food stores. It took many months, but I sold every box.

The following autumn, believe it or not, Gangadhar started getting that craving for Filsinger apples again. But by then the old Queensboro Dairy truck was giving us so much trouble that we had to junk it. Our only other truck was a Datsun pickup, far too small to haul a heavy load of apples. Gangadhar was disappointed that our milk truck was gone, but I was totally relieved!

CHAPTER 11
THE IRS POSTER GIRL

There is one aspect of running even a small company that no one likes to discuss, and that is the finances. Knowing how careful I am about details, Gangadhar turned most of these responsibilities over to me.

In 1974 we needed to secure a loan. The idea of borrowing money was foreign to me; it was practically against my religion. I asked Manny Shemin, our friend and advisor, who he thought I might contact to arrange for a loan, and he suggested a bank called Farm Credit. He explained that as a type of "farm," we might qualify for a low-interest farm loan. I always took Manny's advice, so I made an appointment with the bank that he recommended.

When the bank officer, an old-timer named Mr. Donahue, came to interview me, he asked many questions about our personal finances. I politely informed him that I could not give out that type of information, because my mother had always told me I should keep it confidential.

For some unknown reason, the gentlemanly Mr. Donahue accepted my application without requiring me to divulge any personal information. Farm Credit loaned us $35,000. This loan was called a revolving credit, which meant we could pay it back at any time and take it out again, if needed. This was the perfect arrangement for someone like me. I paid back the money and borrowed it again countless times during the year, because I was so uncomfortable with the idea of owing money.

For 11 years, with my credit limit increasing every year, I was able to secure this type of loan from Farm Credit. It was not until Mr. Donahue retired that I was actually required to fill in the personal side of the application. Now, whenever I have to provide this kind of information, I remember my mother's admonition and do not tell them about all of our valuables. I have taken my mother's advice to heart: Some things should always remain confidential.

And my own piece of advice on the subject of finances is this: Always pay your taxes on time—early is even better. One year my son Durdam said to me, "Mom, you are the IRS Poster Girl. I have never seen anyone so eager to pay their taxes!" It is true. I look at taxes the same way I look at borrowed money—I like to have it paid and off my "To Do" list as soon as possible.

Even the idea of the quarterly estimated tax annoys me. I can't understand why, when you know in April what is going to be due the following January, you can't just pay up and be done with it. Our unfortunate bookkeeper, John Guido, has to have our monthly sales tax computed even before the forms arrive in the mail.

I wish we could be as on-time with all our other office obligations as we are with paying taxes. Preparing monthly bills for clients is a task neither of us enjoys. Gangadhar is horrified when we have to send out big bills. One day Richie, my first worker back in the parking lot of the deli, gave my husband some very practical advice. What he said was, "If you don't like sending out big bills, then don't do big jobs."

Richie, now our full-time employee

CHAPTER 12
KYOTO GARDENS

I cannot remember when my husband first became intrigued with Bonsai. We had a traditional nursery, we were well employed as landscapers, and suddenly Bonsai and all things Japanese began to take over. Perhaps he has a Japanese soul from past incarnations. He surely understands and shares the Japanese love of beauty and perfection. France is everywhere in his independent spirit, but the purity and simplicity of Japanese design fulfils him in a very deep way.

Our first Bonsai purchases were from a small nursery in Ellenville, New York. Gangadhar soon become dissatisfied with their selection of plants. He wanted more authentic Bonsai. When we learned about

Selecting Ficus Bonsai in Taiwan

the Yokohama Nursery, one of the most highly-regarded nurseries in Japan, from the Japanese Consulate, we placed an order for one hundred *Pinus parviflora*, sight unseen.

This first order was doomed. The U.S. Department of Agriculture does not allow the importation of potted plants. The roots must be washed clean and found to be 100% free of foreign soil. So when we received our pine trees, they were bare-root, and we had no idea what type of culture these plants needed. Only twenty trees survived.

After this disappointment, my husband began a series of yearly trips to Japan, where he learned much from the Japanese Bonsai Masters and growers. Our importation of Bonsai continued, and each year we met with more success.

In 1982, when our boys were 12 and 14, we took our first family vacation to Japan. Both Gangadhar and I were marathon runners by then. Because of jet lag, we were wide awake at 2 A.M., and would often go out for our long training runs before daylight. It was during these pre-dawn adventures that we began to assimilate Japanese culture.

We stopped at temples that had begun morning rituals, and walked respectfully through the gardens, observing the caretakers as they prepared for the day. I made sure I always had a tiny camera in my pouch, because if we saw something memorable, we knew we would never be able to find our way back to the same spot later in the day.

Gangadhar had been told by our neighbor, artist Noriko Prince, that the best place to find *Pinus parviflora* was on the Japanese island of Shikoku. Noriko lived across the street from our nursery, which was now called Shanti Bithi ("Path of Peace" in Bengali). She was a close friend of the famed Japanese sculptor, Isamu Noguchi. Noriko arranged for Gangadhar to be received at Noguchi's home and studio, which were on Shikoku.

It was a long trip by train and ferry to get to Shikoku. We decided I would remain with the boys in Kyoto. In the end, Gangadhar was sorry we had not come with him. When he rejoined us in Kyoto he described not only the Noguchi sculptures but also all the uncarved stones in the area. "It was quarry heaven," he said. The island of Shikoku, it turned out, was famous not only for *Pinus parviflora*, but also for its "stone village."

Gangadhar's fascination with and love of stonework was apparent even before this visit to Shikoku. On every trip we took, he found stones that he wanted to bring home. A pearl-white boulder the size of an automobile that he saw on the beach in Viña del Mar, Chile, was the one he wanted most. Gangadhar fantasized for days about getting a permit to export this stone. A natural grouping in a riverbed along the roadside between Jakarta and Samudra Beach, Indonesia, also caught his eye. These enormous, smooth, black stones inspired the same type of longing as the white Chilean boulder.

It was not until he went to Shanghai, during the first year that American businessmen were permitted to visit China, that my husband's lust for beautiful stones was partially satisfied. He purchased a container of Tai Hu and Bamboo Shoot stones. The stone sculpture at our barn, which he created with some of these, was featured in *AD Germany* (the German version of *Architectural Digest*) in November, 2003. In the late fall of 2005, Gangadhar created a similar sculpture on Michael Steinhardt's Bedford, New York property, using 42 Bamboo Shoot stones. A photo of the newly installed sculpture is on the facing page.

Facing page: *Aspiration-Sky* with backdrop of *Larix decidua*

Carpinus koreana (Korean hornbeam) purchased on Jerome's first trip to Korea in 1983.
This specimen is now a part of Shanti Bithi's permanent collection. (Photo © 2004 Lawrence Ivy)

CHAPTER 13
PLANT QUARANTINE

For the first few years, my husband took the business trips to Japan by himself. We both felt that one of us should stay home with the boys and run the nursery. One particular time, however, he begged me to come with him. I agreed, but not without angst. Although our boys were by then in junior high and high school, we had never both been away from them for more than a day or two.

Gangadhar left ahead of me and went first to Korea and Taiwan. These countries were part of his usual itinerary. It was decided that I would join him in Tokyo.

It seemed like Mr. Kishida, from The Yokohama Nursery, introduced us to every Bonsai grower in Saitama Prefecture, just outside Tokyo. We were served green tea at each nursery. Our heads were spinning and our hearts were racing at the end of each

Drinking green tea with Mr. Kishida (center) and Mr. Masui, a Bonsai grower

three cities. The following morning we took an early train to Nagoya for an appointment at Fukukaen Nursery. When we arrived in Nagoya, a grey and industrial city, we checked into a tall nondescript business hotel. We were planning to go out with Mr. Yoshida of Fukukaen that very afternoon.

As soon as we got to our room, Gangadhar picked up the phone to call home. All of a sudden I noticed that the bed he was sitting on was shaking. My first thought was that it was some type of mechanism for massage, and I said, "Turn that off, Gangadhar!"

But he was as surprised as I was. "I didn't touch anything," he replied. "Why is the bed shaking?" Leaving the question unanswered, Gangadhar

day. We had no idea that green tea had so much caffeine in it!

I learned on that trip that you have to beg and plead for the Bonsai you hope to import. While you are sitting on makeshift stools and sipping tea, you begin to "discuss." Mr. Kishida did all the negotiating for us, and he would tell us only after we had left each nursery what they were willing to let us purchase. In all cases, we found out, it was necessary to buy a great many little plants in order to secure even one "specimen."

I caught on to the bargaining techniques quickly, even with the language barrier, and Gangadhar felt that having me along was a definite plus—so much so that twice after that I made the buying trips solo. I am shameless, and I know how to beg.

Gangadhar has a great eye, but he leaves the "deal" more to fate.

By some miracle we persuaded one nursery to sell us six incredible juniper specimens. They were quite costly, but we were thrilled at the prospect of having these *Juniperus chinensis* 'Shimpaku' at Shanti Bithi. They were like no others we had seen for sale, and would be a great addition to our growing collection.

Gangadhar explained to me that the Department of Agriculture would require our newly imported plants to spend two years in quarantine at the nursery before being released for sale. I didn't care about having to wait two years; the Shimpaku junipers were a real find!

Our schedule on this trip was hectic; we only had six days to visit

Posing with a rare *Pinus pentaphylla* grown from seed

hung up the phone. The building was now swaying as if it were going to fall over.

I grabbed my purse and ran out into the hall, where several Japanese women were standing, one in her petticoat. We did not wait to find out what was happening. Shoeless, we raced down fourteen flights of stairs and pushed open the fire door at the bottom of the staircase, setting off the hotel fire alarm. No one else followed us out of the emergency exit. Even in the street, everyone seemed to be going about their business.

When we finally got our bearings, we walked around the corner and back through the front entrance into the lobby of our hotel. It was eerie. Everyone around us seemed so calm, even with the fire alarm ringing incessantly. We were truly embarrassed at having set off the alarm, but we didn't know who to apologize to.

It had been a major earthquake, Mr. Yoshida explained to us later that morning during an aftershock that set the cups and saucers rattling across the coffee shop counter. "The Bullet Train stopped," he told us matter-of-factly. This was an indication that the quake was a major one.

Unused to this type of event, Gangadhar and I were both shaken up for days. But in Japan, business is business, and so we continued our visits to nurseries, where once again cups of green tea and discussions around a small heating stove were the ritual to close every deal.

We left Nagoya and took the long train and ferry to Shikoku. Gangadhar was excited to show me

At Isamu Noguchi's studio on Shikoku Island, Japan

Noguchi's studio with its beautiful stone sculptures. But I could tell that he was more interested in the the stones we could see here and there, that had not yet become sculptures. These untouched stones were not for sale, of course; we didn't even ask.

After six days and a lot of suitcase-dragging through train stations, we left for home on separate planes. Another long solo flight, but the return trip is shorter, and the prospect of seeing my boys made it easier for me.

Back at Shanti Bithi, we anxiously awaited the arrival of all the plants we had purchased. The wait is always unnerving because the plants have to pass inspection by the Department of Agriculture. The inspectors are strict, and can sometimes deny entry to an entire shipment, but we had been lucky of late.

My brother-in-law Didier was working for us at that time. One of his jobs was to see that our plants were released from Customs in a timely fashion. Didier went immediately to Agriculture at JFK when we were notified that the plants had arrived. He secured the release of our six precious Junipers, plus all the smaller Bonsai we had purchased to make the deal. There were 20 boxes in all, he told us when he phoned to say he was on his way home. We were relieved that the plants had been released so quickly.

But when Didier arrived at Shanti Bithi he did not look very happy, and here is why: He had not secured the boxes with ropes, and two boxes had fallen out of the truck along the way. He thought maybe it had happened on the Throgs Neck Bridge.

My brother-in-law's "apology" went something like this: "Well, you have 18 boxes, and I'm sorry, but we're only missing two." I had a sinking feeling.

We off-loaded the shipment as hurriedly as we could to figure out what was missing from the truck, and it was soon apparent that the six beautiful juniper specimens were the ones that had fallen out.

I quietly left the nursery and went home in tears. Compounding my anger and frustration was the feeling that we had broken our trust with the Bonsai Master. He would eventually inquire how his plants were doing, and Mr. Kishida would want to know if they had made it out of Agriculture. What in the world were we going to tell them?

My husband had never seen me so disheartened. He counted on my optimism when things were not going our way. My uncharacteristic silence alarmed him, and he decided to take action.

Gangadhar telephoned the Bridge & Tunnel Authority (BTA) and informed them that quarantined plants had fallen out of our truck, perhaps on the Throgs Neck Bridge. He telephoned Associated Press and told them that he had notified the BTA that quarantined plants

had fallen out of our truck, and if anyone found them, would they kindly notify Shanti Bithi Nursery.

What followed was quite astonishing. Every ten minutes on 1010 WINS and WCBS 880 news radio there was a bulletin about quarantined plants that were missing. Shanti Bithi's name and phone number were broadcast repeatedly.

Eventually the BTA closed the bridge to look for the plants, causing quite a traffic jam. Later that night a call came from the Bridge and Tunnel Authority, informing us that they had found two crushed boxes of plants on the bridge. "We don't know what to do with them," they told us. "Please come and pick them up immediately."

Gangadhar was amused that they seemed afraid they might catch some disease from our "quarantined" plants. But he was not happy that they expected him to drive down to the Bronx in the middle of the night to pick up our now worthless cargo.

The story was not yet over. Early the following morning when we went to work, there on the front lawn of Shanti Bithi Nursery was a news crew with television cameras, waiting to interview us. We looked at each other, realizing that now we would have to face the media and answer a lot of awkward questions. Gangadhar turned to me and said in a hushed voice, "Are you satisfied?"

Now, what did that mean? Was I satisfied because we had gotten so much publicity for our Bonsai nursery as a result of his telephone calls? Or was I quite satisfied

that now he had to answer tricky questions live on television? After all, Didier was his brother, not mine.

Gangadhar had managed to turn things around for us, and I was truly grateful. Once again, my enthusiasm for the nursery business returned.

CHAPTER 14
THE 10,000ᵀᴴ MCDONALD'S

I give my husband all the credit for the good publicity we have had over the years. Most, if not all, of the clever ideas about promoting Shanti Bithi have been his.

During the first gas crisis, he contacted Associated Press and told them that we were offering a 10% discount to customers who came to pick up their Christmas trees on horseback. After *The Wall Street Journal* picked up the story and put it on the front page, several people actually did come on horseback (photo above).

One spring, the weather forecast was for a deep freeze in early April. That day I had unloaded two tractor trailers full of flowering plants and shrubs. Upon hearing the ominous forecast, we stuffed as many plants as we could into our tiny store. The rest of our spring orders had to remain outside overnight and endure the freezing temperatures. Gangadhar had heard that creating a flow of moisture would keep the air temperature warmer, so we decided that we would leave the sprinklers on all night.

The following morning our entire nursery was covered with a sheet of ice! We didn't know what damage we would find when it melted, but it was a beautiful sight. Gangadhar telephoned *The Stamford Advocate*, our local newspaper. The next day, the entire front page was a picture of "Shanti Bithi Under Ice." Luckily, our experiment had, in fact, protected most of the newly-budded plants, and the front-page publicity was no small consolation for the loss of those that did not survive.

In 1986 a friend of ours opened a public relations firm. We wrote a series of articles about our work for him to use. One essay described a tennis court we had designed and installed. To our surprise, in the January, 1987 Holiday Issue of *Playboy Magazine*, which listed "The Best of the Best," Jerome Rocherolle was named as the best tennis court designer in the world. Our tennis court, set at the base of a steep slope, beside a spring-fed pond, features a sculpture of Don Quixote by Nathaniel Kaz standing at mid-court as referee (photo right).

We thought it was hilarious to have made it into *Playboy*. Someone else did not. The Sunday morning after the magazine article appeared, we received an irate telephone call from Mr. R, a prominent landscape architect in the Bedford area. He was actually yelling into the telephone, accusing us of taking credit for one of his tennis court designs. It is true that we had been hired by his client to landscape their tennis court, which Mr. R had designed. But the tennis court that we had described and photographed for the *Playboy Magazine* article was the one we had built in our own backyard.

The following year, we decided to design a display garden for the New York Flower Show. The theme we chose was "East Meets West." We used our own life-sized sculpture of James Joyce by Milton Hebald to represent the "West" in our display garden. He sat at the edge of a forest of cedar trees, contemplating the Bonsai and moss garden we had designed to his right. The "East" and "West" theme gardens were connected by a stepping-stone walkway. For this exhibit, Shanti Bithi won a gold medal from the Chicago Horticultural Society "for outstanding horticultural skill and knowledge."

You never really know who notices your work at these trade shows. A year after the New York Flower Show, a Mr. Y of the Japan Development Corporation phoned us. He had been contracted by a wealthy Japanese businessman to oversee construction of the 10,000th McDonald's Restaurant, in Washington, D.C. Mr. Y's client had seen our exhibit at the

Don Quixote by Nathaniel Kaz

James Joyce by Milton Hebald

architects who had traveled from Japan just for this meeting. We were astonished that these men had come so far to discuss the garden design for a fast-food restaurant.

Our design plans for the McDonald's garden were ultimately accepted. While our client's confidence in us was flattering, and we were being paid extravagant sums for what was still the development phase, the urgent phone calls, the on-site meetings, and the protocol soon became intrusive. We began to have second thoughts about this new relationship.

We also began to realize that it would be difficult to execute our design satisfactorily by supervising outside crews for the construction of the garden. "No problem," said Mr. Y when we informed him of our misgivings. "We will bring Shanti Bithi crews to Washington." There seemed to be no way out.

We were just starting the cost-analysis phase of the project when the client suddenly withdrew his offer to be the franchisee for the 10,000th McDonald's. Apparently, he was not happy with the Four-Corners site that had been proposed. We truly breathed a sigh of relief. Corporate protocol did not suit our informal country ways.

New York Flower Show, and had been so impressed with our design that he wanted us to create the garden for his landmark restaurant.

We were surprised; there are so many Japanese designers and architects available in the U.S. After some preliminary discussions, we arranged an April meeting with Mr. Y at Shanti Bithi Nursery to present our design proposal. Mr. Y brought with him a team of three landscape

Shanti Bithi Nursery display garden, designed by Saeko Oshiro

CHAPTER 15
FIFTY~FIFTY

During one of our yearly meetings with Manny Shemin of Shemin Nurseries, the idea of forming a corporation was discussed. Our business was registered as a partnership at that time, but Manny insisted that our growing company needed the protection of a corporation. So we contacted our local Connecticut attorney, Rob T, and asked him to file the necessary papers.

Months later, when he finally had all the documents ready, Rob mentioned that before we signed, we needed to appoint two officers. There was a short silence; then Gangadhar spoke up. "Okay, I'll be President. It's no big deal. Do you mind if I'm President?" he said to me.

"No," I replied, "but then what will I be?"

"Well, you can be anything else

—the Secretary, the Treasurer, or the Vice-President," Rob offered.

I thought about it for a moment. I decided I didn't like the idea of being Vice-President, so I said, "All right, then I'll be Secretary."

We were about to complete the signing of the documents when Rob casually mentioned, "Oh, by the way, a corporation has shareholders, so we have to assign shares of the company. What do you think, you guys?"

This is where I perked up, because I had had experience with shares of stock in my father's company. Stock has a value; it's worth something. So I said, "Okay, that's easy. Gangadhar will have 49% and I will have 51%. How is that?"

Well, my husband hit the ceiling. "No way! It is fifty-fifty or nothing. We are partners."

"Then why are you President and I'm only Secretary? What makes up for that?"

I was half joking, but he was dead serious. I was teasing the Archie Bunker side of him, but maybe I wasn't joking all that much. Perhaps I really did want the bigger half. Anyway, it didn't matter, because he made it quite clear that I wasn't getting it.

CHAPTER 16
NO BIG DEAL

Each year, as soon as we heard where our winter holiday was going to be, I immediately did one thing: I went to the New Canaan Book Shop and purchased several books about the countries that were on our proposed itinerary. These trips were arranged by our meditation group, and even though I dreaded traveling to Third World countries, I usually went, and was often pleasantly surprised. As for the books, I don't know why I wasted my money on travel guides, because I only read the sections entitled "Travel Precautions."

One year we were planning to visit Indonesia. In my selected chapter there was everything I did not like:

1) Don't drink the water (i.e., use Evian even for shampooing).

2) Be careful of the food (i.e., do not eat anything that you didn't bring from home).

3) Beware of malarial mosquitoes (i.e., do not leave your room).

Add to that the long airplane trip, and I was not looking forward to any of it.

In this particular instance, my expectations proved to be correct. One of the places we visited on this trip was called Padang. Padang had open sewers and an infestation of rats, both indoors and out. Even my supplies of matzoh, peanut butter, bags of small tootsie rolls (seven per day), and cans of tuna fish (which I bring but never open because I am a vegetarian—the tuna fish is in case I decide to become un-vegetarian) were not enough to lift my spirits. I barely left my room, and I was not a happy camper.

But I survived, as usual. And on the way home we made a stop in Tokyo. Visiting Japan was something I always looked forward to on trips to Asia—this time more than ever!

Gangadhar and I left Indonesia on separate planes and arranged to meet for two days in Tokyo. One day was for going to Bonsai nurseries with Mr. Kishida, and the other day was for shopping. We selected some plants, but since Gangadhar was planning to make a detour to Korea, we decided to ship the boxes of Bonsai to our nursery, instead of checking them with our luggage, as we usually did. Also, I had to clear customs in Seattle and then change to a domestic flight home.

Mr. Kishida was happy to spend the day with us. He always offered us a thoughtful gift whenever we came. This time, his gift was a small Bonsai apple tree. Gangadhar was intrigued by the tiny apples that hung from the branches.

When we arrived back in our hotel the night before my return flight, I said to him, "What are we going to do with this tree? I can't take it with me."

"Why not?" he replied. "It's so tiny. I'll pack it up in a box and you can just check it with your luggage. It weighs nothing."

"That's not the point," I said. "I won't have time to go to Agriculture in Seattle because I only have two hours between flights."

"You can skip Agriculture. I'll just pack it in a box and you won't declare it."

"I'm not doing that," I protested. "I am not smuggling in any plants. What if they ask me questions when I go through customs?"

"I have a great idea," said Gangadhar. "I'll pack it in a box addressed to Granny and Bon Pappy at La Rocherolle. If they ask, just say your husband gave it to you and it's for his parents. You don't even have to say you know what it is," he instructed.

"No, I'm not going to be bothered with that plant."

"It's not a big deal, I tell you. We have a license to import plants." He was becoming frustrated with me and he kept insisting that I had nothing to worry about.

Well, he was wrong. First of all, I worried about that box during the entire flight. And when I deplaned and picked up my luggage to pass through customs I was getting more and more anxious. "Why did I let him talk me into this?" I wondered.

When my turn came, the agent asked me what I did, and that was where I made a big mistake. I said, "I work." I don't know why I said that. I usually say I'm a housewife. But this time I gave a stupid answer, and the question that followed sank my ship. They asked where I worked and I said, "At a nursery."

PLANTS are at nurseries! That was a bad answer. Right away I was sent to the red line where you bring your luggage for inspection. I was sick to my stomach. All I had on my cart was one suitcase and one box. I thought of taking the box off the cart and just leaving it, but in big letters on the front and back was written:

M. ET MME ROCHEROLLE
CHÂTEAU DE LA ROCHEROLLE
INDRE, FRANCE

Once you pass the first customs station and are motioned into the red line, all eyes are upon you. My heart was racing. It was too late to rearrange the cart and put the box on the bottom. That would only make me more suspect. So I proceeded to the counter with all the color drained from my face, and of course the first thing they asked me was, "What's in the box?"

I was trembling by then, and I mumbled, "I'm not sure. It's for my husband's parents."

Oh my God! I had barely finished answering the question when the inspector began to open the box. It was full of crumpled newspaper, and

I hoped he wouldn't find anything. But he dug his hand down and triumphantly pulled out the tiny apple tree.

"This is a fruit tree!" the inspector began to shout at me. "You didn't <u>know</u> this was in the box? How could you bring this into the country? This could ruin the entire apple crop in Washington State!" He was so ferocious you would have thought I had brought in the atom bomb.

I was too frightened to think about the substance of what he was saying. I began to cry, but he did not care one bit about my tears. He held up that tiny little tree to show the other inspectors, saying, "Look at this! Look what I found!" I felt like everyone was looking at <u>me</u>, the criminal, as the inspector gloated over his contraband.

Then he tore through the rest of my luggage and dumped everything out of my purse onto the counter. I was sobbing, but he continued to be so abusive that I was terrified he was going to arrest me.

Fortunately, there was a female customs officer working behind the same counter, who took pity on me. As soon as the agent finished searching through my things, she told him that she would take care of the rest. When I had stuffed my jumbled belongings back into the suitcase, she took me by the arm and walked me over to the counter where fines are paid. My fine was only $100. The female officer waited with me while I tearfully fumbled through my purse, wondering what was next.

To my surprise, she offered to escort me through some private corridors so that I would not miss my flight to New York. I was grateful to her, but I was still shaking.

I hesitated before boarding the plane. I really wanted to call my husband and yell at him for saying it was no big deal. I was sure that he knew fruit trees are something you cannot import, even with a license. He knew which plants were on the U.S.D.A. "prohibited" list, so he must have deliberately forgotten to mention that Agriculture would have confiscated this plant under any circumstances.

I thought about how carefully he had washed the soil off the roots of that Bonsai tree in the sink of our pristine Akasaka Prince Hotel bathroom. I decided I would need more time than an airport telephone call to scold him, so I boarded the plane. What a scoundrel. And all because of those tiny apples!

Maple Forest Bonsai on a slab, designed and planted at Shanti Bithi Nursery by our Bonsai expert, Saeko Oshiro.
This forest has been featured at the New York Botanical Garden's annual fall exhibit entitled:
Momijigari: The Japanese Autumn Garden.

CHAPTER 17
SAYING NO

A gentleman named Michael Steinhardt, who would later become much more than a customer, visited Shanti Bithi in the early 1980s to purchase a Bonsai tree for his New York City apartment. Despite his insistence and pleadings, we refused to sell him one of our big, beautiful and costly specimens. We just didn't think he would be able to care for it properly. In fact, we knew that even the most experienced plantsman would have difficulty nurturing a Bonsai on a windy, sooty New York terrace. And so we just said no.

It was not an auspicious beginning to a long collaboration. And years later we forgot how to say that word with the same conviction and freedom.

A year or two after Michael's visit to Shanti Bithi, we received an excited phone call from his wife, Judy, whom we had never met, telling us about a fresh herb business that she and Michael had just begun. It had been written up in *The New York Times*. Judy was bubbling with childlike enthusiasm.

We were confused by this out-of-the-blue telephone conversation. We didn't really understand why Judy was contacting us. This was our private thought, which we didn't want to think out loud. Judy is intuitive, however, and she immediately added, "Someday we are going to do something with you, I just know it. I don't know what it is, but something." Click.

In 1985 Judy contacted us to help with the design of her terrace in New York City. Gangadhar is not a put-it-on-paper communicative artist. He knows exactly what he wants—so much so that once he has the vision in his mind's eye, he often feels that his work is completed. But this was a New York City cooperative building with boards and rules. A design had to be submitted on paper.

We asked our friend Noriko Prince to do conceptual drawings for us, and she agreed. We mailed Judy the three drawings, along with our recommendations, but this project never materialized.

Once again years passed, and then one day in early spring Judy contacted Gangadhar, requesting him to come over to their Bedford property. The Steinhardts had been working with an English landscape designer and wanted Jerome, as Judy calls him, to prune some maple trees on a mostly barren north-facing slope opposite their home. Judy thought that with his expertise in Bonsai and Japanese design, my husband could do something small and contained on this northern slope.

Shortly thereafter, Gangadhar asked me to come to the Steinhardts' and walk the hillside with him. I wasn't concentrating on the slope, because there was not much there to see. What I couldn't stop looking at was hundreds and hundreds of plants in containers under some trees at the bottom of the slope—almost more than we had for sale in our entire nursery.

When I asked Gangadhar about the plants under the trees, he said, "They have an English landscape designer, and I don't know if things are going that well, but it has nothing to do with us, absolutely nothing! Let's concentrate on this hill. That's all they asked us to do."

"Okay, okay."

CHAPTER 18
GETTING STARTED

In the spring of 1988 our company was running so many different job sites that I hardly saw my husband at all during the day. Easter is always "crunch time" for nurseries. Everyone wants their gardens to look beautiful as soon as the weather gets warm, so I was busy, Gangadhar was busy, and our nursery was busy—not only with Bonsai, but also with selling flowers and landscape plants. I was designing perennial gardens and flower pots for my own clients as well as for Gangadhar's clients. It was only during the evening hours that my husband and I found time to visit job sites together and quietly consult with one another.

On April 17, 1988 Shanti Bithi sent nine men to Michael and Judy Steinhardt's estate in Bedford, New York. Within weeks of getting started on the hillside that we had walked together only the previous month, we were already considering several new projects that the Steinhardts had discussed with us. Even so, we saw this as just another big job. A new one always seemed to miraculously appear when the present one was winding down.

There was not much open space on the Steinhardts' property.

Gangadhar wanted to create vistas and open views to the main pond and the hillside beyond. That meant taking down some trees that were either weak or "unimportant," but it was not clear-cutting. We always try to preserve old trees that have established their place on the property.

While our landscaping crews were clearing views at this new job site, our masons were repairing old stone walls and building new ones. These walls became an integral part of the garden structure. (Ten years after we began working there, Shanti Bithi had built more than two miles of walls on the Steinhardts' property.)

In late spring of 1989, Gangadhar began noticing some beautiful stones that were being excavated during the renovation of the Hutchinson River Parkway. Every time we drove by these piles of stones, he practically ran us off the road. "Did you see those stones?" he would say for the umpteenth time.

"Yes, I see them," I would reply.

Finally, one day he pulled off the parkway and made a deal with the construction foreman, who agreed to sell us stones by the truckload. We returned for load after load of Hutchinson River Parkway stones, which we used for the first stepping-stone walkway on the Steinhardts' property (photo facing page).

During a long training run one morning, we discovered that a large tract of land near our nursery was about to be developed. This site was littered with moss-covered boulders of every imaginable size and shape. To ensure that the most beautiful and interesting stones went into our trucks, we often arrived at the construction site before 6 A.M. and marked the ones we wanted.

Our most difficult challenge in the early years on the Steinhardt project was the approximately fifty cultivars of *Acer palmatum* (Japanese maple) that had been planted on a north slope, orchard style, by the previous landscaper. We wanted to naturalize these trees and create a garden out of what was now simply a plant collection.

Gangadhar pruned the maples to give them character, but some were mere saplings and needed time to grow. We decided to wait before transplanting them into a garden setting. We did not wait, however, to begin scouring the country for new cultivars and larger specimens.

Another early project we embarked on was the design and construction of a moss-covered bridge on the north slope (photo page 54). That same spring we began redesigning the Main Pond, setting weathered boulders so that it would look like it had always been there (photos page 53).

When renovation of the Main Pond was completed, we began designing a Fern Garden. To prevent soil erosion on the steep hillside, we planted hundreds, if not thousands, of *Polystichum acrostichoides* (Christmas Ferns), a native species. Once the hillside was stabilized, we began adding unusual varieties.

In those early years we also focused a great deal of our attention on developing the Woodland Garden. This garden, featuring plants that ostensibly thrive in shade, is set under a grove of large *Leriodendron tulipifera* (Tulip trees) whose branches begin 50 feet above the ground. We planted *Hydrangea anomala* ssp. *petiolaris* (Climbing hydrangea) in the early 1990s. They now reach these lower branches and beyond.

We also gave importance to the understory trees and shrubs. We collected *Azalea mucronulatum* and naturalized them into the Woodland Garden. When we purchased a named cultivar, such as 'Cornell Pink,' we pruned out 50% of the branches to help speed up the naturalized look. This native species blooms in early spring, often when there is still snow on the ground (page 52, lower center).

In summer the Woodland Garden becomes lush with *Hydrangea quercifolia* (Oakleaf Hydrangea),

The Allée wall

Stone landing at the Fern Pond

other is *Betula jacquemontii*, whose white bark is visible at night (Table of Contents pages). Opposite these groves, along a stream that feeds into the west end of the Main Pond, we also began a Grass Garden (below, right).

During those first few years Shanti Bithi often sent more than 25 of our workers to the Steinhardt property. With both our boys now away at college, my husband and I were unmindful of how much the scope of this job was consuming our time and energy. Without noticing it, we were becoming addicted to designing and developing this exciting garden.

One morning in the spring of 1991, the Steinhardts' longtime housekeeper, Gertrude, told Gangadhar that she wanted to see me. Gertrude was my favorite "Steinhardt." The sight of her in the kitchen used to take away my exhaustion on a hot summer day. She reminded me of our housekeeper, Sylvia (whom I called "Swilly"), back in Kings Point. Swilly filled my teen years with extra affection, along with stories of her

Hydrangea arborescens 'Annabelle,' a species with beautiful pale green turning-to-white flowers, Hostas, and the very invasive *Matteuchia struthiopteris* (Ostrich ferns).

Along the banks of the Main Pond, we planted two groves of trees in the early years. One is *Betula nigra* 'Heritage' with its beautiful exfoliating bark (lower left); the

life, and hilarious imitations of some of the guests my dad used to bring home for dinner.

When I went up to the house, Gertrude happened to be outside. She greeted me, as always, with tremendous affection, and then got right to the point.

"Are ya takin' video, darlin'?" she asked with her almost incomprehensible Jamaican accent.

"Yes, Gertrude, I'm taking pictures." I answered.

"No, darlin,' I mean, are ya takin' video?"

I didn't understand, for a moment, what she was saying. Seeing that I was perplexed, she continued, "Yas workin' sa hard, you 'n him. Yas shed be takin' video. Them not gon' rememba what yas did."

Now I understood where she was going. I took Gertrude's admonition to heart, as I would have taken anything Swilly had said to me. From that day forward I began documenting the development of all the gardens with much greater care.

Above and right:
The Main Pond during and after redesign

Page 51:
Iberis sempervirens 'Little Gem' and
Tulip *backeri* 'Lilac Wonder'

Left:
The Moss Bridge, which has a view of the Main Pond. *Hydrangea anomala* ssp. *petiolaris* climbs the trunks of two largeTulip trees in the foreground.

Facing page:
Hostas and purple-flowering *Ajuga pyramidalis* bordering a pine-needle walkway, with Japanese iris and *Matteuchia struthiopteris* (Ostrich ferns) behind them at the edge of the pond.

Far left:
Sanguinaria canadensis 'Multiplex'

Left:
Euphorbia polychroma

Above and upper and lower right:
Helleborus x hybridus 'Royal Heritage'

Center right:
Helleborus x hybridus 'White Strain'

Facing page:
Martha, an elegant Blue Crane, takes a stroll in the Maple Garden

Overleaf:
Phlox stolonifera 'Bruce's White' and 'Blue Ridge',
with *Polystichum acrostichoides* (Christmas ferns)

CHAPTER 19

BORROWED LANDSCAPE

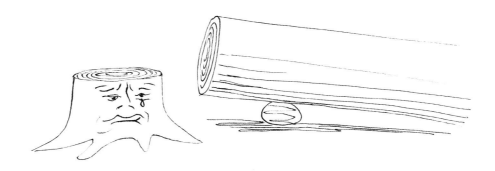

Clearing vistas and creating views is an obsession with my husband. The first thing he sees when we visit a property is what is obstructing a view and which trees are no longer necessary. From a design perspective, he is always correct, but I have a much harder time making this kind of decision. Sometimes he tells me, "That tree has to go; it is very weak," and when I look at the tree he is referring to, it doesn't always appear to be weak. But I never have the chance to know for sure, because the next day that "weak" tree is gone.

Since our boys were little, they have always loved trees. Their favorite childhood storybook was *The Giving Tree*, and their most sacred summer ritual was climbing the Mulberry tree in our front yard to feast on the berries. My boys are horrified that their father has cut down even a single tree, and often tease him, saying that when he goes to Heaven he will be in full sun all the time because of the trees he has cut down over the years.

Gangadhar's love of vistas sometimes extends even beyond the boundaries of the property he is landscaping. One time he got permission from a neighbor of the Steinhardts to cut down six dead or dying ash trees on the neighbor's

property. Shortly thereafter, the unhappy neighbor telephoned and asked for a meeting with Michael and Judy. Apparently my husband had cut down 21 ash trees! Gangadhar was invited to attend this meeting to defend himself.

The meeting did not go well. The neighbors accused Gangadhar of cutting down more trees than they had agreed to. His defense was that the trees were dead or dying. Still, they could not understand why he had taken down 21 trees when they had only given him permission to cut six. Puzzled, they finally asked Michael how he had let this happen. Michael's reply was, "Nobody can control Jerome."

Several years later these neighbors had to take down more dead and dying ash trees in the same area, this time at their own expense.

CHAPTER 20
THE MAPLE GARDEN

When we started working at Croton Lake Road, the 50 Japanese maples *(Acer palmatum)* that were planted on the North slope looked like a science experiment, not a garden. Gangadhar was intent on bringing in much-needed light to improve the growing conditions. So we began by pruning up the lower branches of the indigenous trees to raise the canopy. Then we set walk-ways and weathered boulders, built bridges and a series of ponds—all to create structure before beginning to transplant the young maples.

We wanted this to be a spiritual garden—meditative, serene and in-spiring. A garden is only a moment, an opportunity that will never come back. It is ever-changing, and it is never finished. You can visit a garden at seven in the morning and have one experience. Hours later, your experience may be entirely different. Flowers open, they close, the petals fall, the wind blows, the light changes. And all these small variations are reflected in the feelings that you have.

Gangadhar's vision was not to emphasize the differences between the many maple cultivars, but to create a series of harmonious groves. One area is dedicated to the dwarf varieties and one to the *japonicum*. The *linearlobum* are grouped together, and there are clusters of red varieties interspersed on the giant hillside. The spring colors, subtle and full of promise, are, in their own way, as dramatic as the fall colors.

Twice a year—once in August and again in late February—each maple tree needs expert pruning to retain its distinctive character. In late November, after the spectacular fall show is over and the trees are bare, every Japanese maple has its trunk and main branches individually wrapped in straw and burlap for winter protection (see page 143).

To prevent washouts on the maple hillside, we planted shade-tolerant groundcovers whose tiny flowers shimmer in the filtered light. Where moss grew naturally, we nurtured it, and we also began transplanting moss from other woodland areas. This was to be our signature groundcover.

As early as spring, 1990, we began searching the country for new maple cultivars. Gangadhar and I visited the late J. D. Vertrees, author of *Japanese Maples*, in Oregon. He told us that the nurseries in Oregon and Washington State would be our best sources in the U.S. During the same period, we placed an order with Firma C. Esveld, the leading European propagator of Japanese maples. We were also fortunate to be able to purchase a number of large and rare varieties from the late Richard Wolff, owner of Red Maple Nursery. He was one of the early growers who specialized in *Acer palmatum*.

One day, while on a marathon training run in Westport, my husband spotted a beautiful old *Acer palmatum dissectum* (cutleaf weeping Japanese maple). He was so excited that he went right up to the house and knocked on the front door. The elderly gentleman who lived there was not interested in selling the tree for money, but said that he would consider letting us have it if we agreed to do yard work for him. A few weeks later a deal was struck. This century-old tree was as wide as it was tall, but the transplant was a success. It is thriving on a hillside at the entry to the Maple Garden, and features in many of our beautiful Maple Garden photos (pages 114 and 117).

By 1994 we had acquired so many new cultivars that we needed to expand the Maple Garden. The newly developed maple planting areas also became the repository for Michael's collection of *Arisaema, Cyprepedium*, and *Podophyllum peltatum*. These delicate and costly specimens, with unusual and striking leaflets and spathes, are grown in a shade house (see page 72) before being transplanted into the gardens.

Although the development of the Maple Garden has been our biggest challenge, it has also been most rewarding. The extraordinary diversity of the *Acer* genus makes the viewing of this collection a visual feast in all seasons.

The Steinhardt Maple collection now has more than 400 cultivars from around the world. For a listing of cultivars and sources, see pages 168–172.

Late October in the Steinhardt Maple Garden

Previous page:
Acer palmatum 'Beni tsukasa'

Above:
Acer palmatum 'Kasagi yama'

Right:
Acer palmatum 'Monzukushi'

Above:
Acer palmatum 'Komachi hime'

Below:
Acer palmatum 'Tsuma gaki'

Left:
Acer palmatum 'Sharp's Pygmy'

Below:
Acer circinatum 'Sunglow'

Right:
Acer palmatum 'Umegae'

Far right:
Acer palmatum dissectum
'Irish Lace'

Facing page top:
Acer palmatum dissectum
'Viridis'

Right:
Acer palmatum 'Variegatum'

Far right:
Acer palmatum 'Butterfly'

Right:
Acer palmatum 'Kiyohime'

Far right:
Acer shirasawanum

Facing page bottom:
Acer japonicum 'Itaya'

Right:
Acer palmatum 'Orange Dream'

Far right:
Acer palmatum acontifolium
'Maiku jaku'

CHAPTER 21
MAIL~ORDER MADNESS

Facing page:
Hemerocallis 'Emperor's Choice' and 'Beautiful Edging,' with *Gaillardia* interspersed

For the first five years that we worked on the Steinhardt estate, building the gardens, ponds, waterfalls, walkways, and bridges had been our main focus. We were also planting at the same time, but only in selected areas. Every time Michael brought up the subject of plants, Gangadhar told him we didn't want to be overwhelmed.

In the autumn of 1994 Michael politely asked permission to put together an order for some plants from the many catalogues he had written away for. It sounded like a simple request, so Gangadhar said to go ahead. Michael came up to me one day, as excited as a child. It was a side of him I had never seen. "Jerome told me I could order anything I want," he informed me. And so he did.

Oh my God! Michael began sending us catalog after catalog in which he had circled practically every plant on each page, ordering at least three of each. That year 2,700 mail-order plants arrived at Croton Lake Road and Shanti Bithi Nursery.

Many mail-order plants, as we learned, are tiny and newly-rooted. Since they were too fragile to be planted directly into the gardens, we were faced with an entirely new challenge.

This was the year Michael and Judy's only daughter, Sara, was getting married, and we had undertaken to do many plantings for the outdoor ceremony. We knew that the entire property had to look perfect for the wedding on June 11th. The deluge of new mail-order plants was about to put us over the edge.

Gangadhar began to panic. In order to calm him down, I came up with a pretty good idea. I suggested that we cut out beds near the barn and grow the new plants there to observe what we had. Gangadhar

designed and cut out a series of beds that were mostly rectangles of varying lengths on both sides of the service road. He also made a special circular bed just for the Alpine plants, where he placed stones to simulate an Alpine setting.

We carefully labeled everything as we planted, but Michael's flock of guinea hens often pecked at the white plastic labels. As a result, some of the plants became nameless. (Our present experimental beds have double labels for each plant—one is buried deep in the soil.) We filled all the experimental beds with a special soil purchased from McEnroe Organics, amending the soil for the Alpine bed as needed. This organic soil was very costly, but the new plants did so well in all the experimental beds that sometimes they were ready to be incorporated into the gardens within a year.

Although the mail-order madness threw us off for a short time, the opportunity to observe such a variety of unusual plants from many different sources was a tremendous boon for us. Our level of plant expertise began to skyrocket. Myron Porto, our horticulturist, studied and nurtured the tiny new plants. I became familiar with the Latin nomenclature because it was my responsibility to make the labels and set them out.

Michael continues to enjoy circling plants in catalogs. In 2003 he ordered 1,800 mail-order plants, enclosing an apologetic note with the stack of catalogs. During the winter months, with more time on our hands, we argue over what to eliminate from these orders. Myron and I are on Michael's side. My husband is the minimalist. "Where are we going to plant all these?" That is his mantra.

Left:
New shade house for shade-loving experimental plants

Facing page:
Hemerocallis 'Becky Sharp'
Some of the experimental beds, like this one, became the permanent home for our *Hemerocallis* collection

See page 166 for a list of our mail-order sources.

Upper Left:
Don Shadow (holding notebook) with
(from left) Myron, Jerome's sister
Caroline Rocherolle, Michael, and
Jerome at the Experimental Gardens

Left:
Judy and Michael Steinhardt at an
interview for the *Financial Times*
(London).
Photo by Pascal Perrich

Facing page:
Hemerocallis 'Going Dancing' in the
foreground
Hydrangea macrophylla 'Veitchii' behind
the wall in full flower
These beds also began as experimental
planting areas.

CHAPTER 22
GARDEN WEDDING

Judy and Michael had a huge gathering at their home to announce the engagement of their only daughter, Sara, to David Berman. Judy began to plan for the wedding at once. My sister-in-law Caroline (now our garden designer) and I were excited that there would be a wedding, and relieved that we would have a year to prepare for the occasion. Gangadhar was less than helpful from the start. He suspected there would be a lot of emotional undercurrents, and he was prepared to stay out of it.

In the beginning there was discussion of having a more informal country wedding. But Judy took charge. She hired a highly reputable party planner whom Gangadhar referred to as "the wedding man," and worked closely with him to make all the arrangements.

Caroline and I lobbied as delicately as we could for an outdoor ceremony at the Dreiser Ruins, because the setting was so romantic. "The Ruins" is an area of the property that had once belonged to Theodore Dreiser, author of *An American Tragedy*. We had torn down his former summer residence, which had fallen into disrepair, but left the stone walls and fireplaces intact to create a garden folly (photo page 81).

Judy ultimately agreed that a ceremony at The Ruins would be beautiful, but she did have some reservations. Because she did not want the stress of worrying about the weather, she arranged to have an enormous tent set up for the reception on the other side of the property. This tent could also be used for the ceremony in case of bad weather.

Caroline and I decided that a mass planting of blue and white *Delphinium* would be beautiful at The Ruins. We contacted several nurseries, and all but Nabels in Mamaroneck refused to grow these plants for us. "Too much trouble," was everyone's response. Nabels intimated that they might have to charge us as much as $150 a pot to promise flowers for a specific date,

so we decided to be frugal and grow them ourselves.

In retrospect, we should have read something into all the refusals, but we chose not to. We purchased cuttings and began setting up our nursery to grow 350 *Delphinium*. In this matter also, Gangadhar was not supportive, but we ignored him. In fact, in most matters of the wedding, Caroline and I became very assertive and independent.

Our *Delphinium* grew beautifully, but they were about to peak two weeks too early. We gave them some hormones to slow their growth, which worked. The flowers were perfect for June 11th. This was just good luck. We were inexperienced greenhouse growers and easily could have found ourselves with nothing to plant for this important occasion.

We were more careful with all the other wedding plantings. Although we seeded the fields surrounding the garden at The Ruins with a wildflower mix, we also used plenty of backup: 400 *Leucanthemum* 'Superbum' and 'Super Alaska', and 350 *Leucanthemum* 'May Queen' and 'Starburst.' The fields were a sea of white flowers. To accent the daisies, we spotted 500 Iceland Poppies for color in the fields closest to where the bride would enter the garden.

All of us listened anxiously to the weather forecasts as the day approached. Caroline and I decided we should wait until the last possible moment to plant the *Delphinium* in the beds, as they were the most important part of our design. For several days before the wedding, the forecast was for on-again, off-again thunderstorms, and so we waited and worried.

The day before the wedding we knew we had no choice but to move the plants from the safe haven of our nursery to the gardens at The Ruins. The weather forecast was still not good, but we were down to the wire. It was a hot and humid day, and we knew that planting the *Delphinium* in beds that were in full sun would make them droop. Our solution was to borrow all of Judy's golf umbrellas, and stake them into the ground to shade the plants.

Left:
Delphinium elatum 'Blue Bird,' 'Blue Jay,' and 'Summer Skies' with old-fashioned roses. Michael escorted his daughter through the Peacock Gate and fields of wildflowers beyond.

This was a plan that should have worked but for the sudden wind that began picking up and moving dark thunderclouds in our direction. It was 7 P.M. on the eve of the wedding when we finished planting, and we now had to make a crucial decision. Should we leave the umbrellas to protect the plants from the heavy rain that was about to come down, or remove them for fear the high winds bringing in the storm would knock the umbrellas down onto our plants? We decided that leaving the umbrellas was more of a hazard, so we took them down. We left for home that evening not knowing whether or not we had made the right decision.

Caroline and I had obsessed so much about planting the *Delphinium* that we were forced to do the entire clean-up ourselves on the morning of the ceremony, and all without Mr. Gangadhar's help. He had spent the three days prior to the wedding on a tractor in the newly expanded Maple Garden, setting a walkway. He stayed as far away from the wedding preparations as he could.

Facing page:
A view of The Ruins
in a field of daisies.

CHAPTER 23
TEAMWORK

In June of 1996, on the first anniversary of Sara and David's wedding, Judy invited us for a quiet dinner at The Ruins to reminisce about how beautiful it had been the year before. We looked out at the fields, the lone wooden barn, and the monkey house that Gangadhar and Joe D'Addona, the caretaker, had designed and built for Fred and Ginger, the spider monkeys. The peacocks were showing off, as they had done for the wedding. It was a serene and beautiful sight.

We had spent a normal busy spring designing and planting. It was unremarkable except for the interviews that Michael and Judy were having with different architects regarding the construction of a guest lodge and some new barns for Michael's growing collection of animals.

Facing page:
Rosea x *alba* 'Maxima'

The Steinhardts chose a prestigious architectural firm to design their new buildings. The principal architect was Mr. T, a senior partner, who had formerly been a dean of architecture at a renowned university. His visits to the site were few and far between, unlike architects we had worked with in the past. He was an elderly gentleman, and we supposed that his aloof manner was a reflection of the way he was as a lecturer.

On September 11, 1996 we received a fax in our office from the project manager overseeing the construction of the guest lodge and service buildings. To paraphrase, the fax said, "Get your plants and related equipment out of said area by October first. If you cannot meet this deadline, please inform, etc., etc., etc." Well, the area he was referring to included all the beds of experimental plants that Michael had ordered during the previous year.

These plantings, near the old barn, had been such a success that we had decided to keep them as a permanent feature of the estate. In fact, we had already named them The Experimental Gardens. Also in this area were several hundred trees and shrubs heeled in and waiting to be sited in beds and gardens that had not yet been created. Was this ever a wake-up call!

We wondered why the project manager had sent us a fax instead of speaking to us personally. We saw him on site every day; he could have easily mentioned it. However, construction was going to begin, and all these things would have to be relocated sooner or later. We resigned ourselves to the inevitable, and began digging up and moving the hundreds and hundreds of plants.

The area that Gangadhar had designed and prepared to be an Alpine Garden happened to be ready at that time, so our first step was to transplant everything that was remotely Alpine in nature into this new space (photo below). The rest we brought back to our nursery hoop houses for winter protection. Those that did not survive the premature transplanting went to plant heaven.

Although we eventually got used to the construction chaos, the formalities always tried our patience. We found the endless memos, faxes and lengthy meetings unproductive and time-consuming. It wasn't how we were used to working. Our focus was always on getting things done in the most expeditious way.

When the new guest lodge was near completion, we were asked to begin our work in the area. A cement bunker housing the central air-conditioning units had been sited

The Alpine Garden

opposite the front door and in full view of the kitchen window. It was the Steinhardts' caretaker, Joe, who brought this to our attention. He saw to it that these units were relocated away from the house and out of sight. We used the newly reclaimed area to plant a grove of fragrant *Chionanthus virginicus* (Fringe trees) and a colorful wildflower garden.

The lodge was difficult to landscape. It was set against a rock ledge and had an undefined front entrance. We began by uncovering and chiseling the ledge (photo next page), creating a striking backdrop for an intimate garden of Alpine plants. Since the rear of the lodge was in a woodland setting, we utilized many of the plants that now thrived in the original Woodland Garden.

A shortage of parking for the many guests that Michael and Judy love to invite also had to be remedied. We solved this problem by creating a guest parking area that could not be seen from the lodge, yet was only a short walk along a path through a field of Sheep's Fescue. The Fescue is dotted with blue *Muscari* (below, left) or colorful wildflowers (this page), depending on the season.

Caroline Rocherolle (right) after prepping a field of wildflowers for an early morning photo shoot.

One afternoon, at what was considered the end of the construction phase, Judy arranged a luncheon for her team of architects and designers. Our plantings were finished for the lodge, as well as for the paddocks adjacent to the new barns. On that particular day, everything on the property was glorious, with masses of wildflowers that we had planted blooming along the drive to the lodge.

As everyone was leaving the luncheon, I noticed that Mr. T made a comment to my husband.

"What did he say to you?" I asked Gangadhar the second I had a chance.

"Nothing really," he replied. "He just said, 'I see that your hand is in everything.' That's all. I guess that was a compliment. Anyway, who cares?" he added, before I could even respond. "The place looks beautiful."

"Yes, it does." I agreed.

But Mr. T is not a team player, I thought to myself as we walked to our car.

Photos left:
Kalmia latifolia 'Sarah' (Mountain laurel) in foreground,
Chionanthus virginicus (Fringe tree) behind rock ledge
Against the house are:
Rhododendron atlanticum 'Choice Creation,'
Rhododendron vaseyii 'White Find,' and
Rhododendron calendulaceum
Flowering groundcover is *Laurentia fluviatilis* 'Solenopsis'

Facing page:
Pinus wallichiana 'Zebrina' (Variegated Himalayan Pine)
planted in the paddocks

Previous page:
Muscari 'Armeniacum'
Gaillardia x grandiflora 'Dazzler,' *Rudbeckia hirta* 'Indian Summer' and 'Prairie Sun,'
Nepeta siberica 'Souvenir d'André Chaudron,'
Agastache 'Blue Fountain,' *Buddleia* 'Ellen's Blue,' *Salvia mexicana* 'Tula,' *Salvia* 'Indigo Spires,' and *Salvia guaranitica, Heliopsis helianthoides* 'Prairie Sunset,' and *Helianthus* 'Moulin Rouge'

A WALK THROUGH THE GARDENS

CHAPTER 24
HURRICANE FLOYD

Michael Steinhardt's passion for plants is matched only by his love of exotic animals and waterfowl. When we first began working at his estate, there was only one horse and one donkey. Today there are African antelopes, albino wallabies, lemurs, marmosets, zebras, camels, capybaras, and many other unusual animals.

After the new barns were completed, it was left to us to landscape the paddocks for these animals. We quickly found that no plant is animal-proof. All the plantings that we have done for the paddocks have to be protected by electric wire, and all the trees are wrapped with protective mesh to prevent the animals from rubbing against them or snacking on the bark and leaves. Even a mass planting of 50 *Ponicirus trifoliata* 'Flying Dragon,' with its ferocious 3-inch thorns (photo right), was devoured by the animals within days.

We have grown accustomed to working side by side with these animals, but from time to time problems arise. One time a longhorn bull jumped the fence and charged through the Experimental Gardens. It took several brave workers to capture him, and he did a lot of damage to the plantings.

At least once a year, a spotted deer manages to escape the confines of its paddock. Sometimes it takes us days to find him. The nibbling on the plants is always an indication of where he has been, but he is difficult to catch. Bar-head geese, guinea hens, and peacocks all roam freely in the gardens. The plant labels and the plants themselves are always at risk.

In the late 1990s we began designing a preserve for Michael's growing collection of exotic ducks.

The first attempt at introducing ducks into the preserve was not a great success. Because they had all been pinioned, the ducks were easy prey for local predators. To solve this problem a protective netting was installed. This area soon became a favorite with Michael and Judy. We began calling it "duck heaven."

Left:
Michael studying his ducks

Below:
Upper pond with *Amelanchier* in bloom

At the end of the day on September 16, 1999, we noted on our worksheet: "Checked property to make sure all catch basins are clear as Hurricane Floyd approaches." The forecast was for heavy rains and damaging winds.

The following morning we drove to Croton Lake Road to see if any trees had come down. Near the entrance to the Steinhardt property, we were forced to stop because a wide section of Croton Lake Road had collapsed, leaving a gaping hole where the road had been. We parked our car on the side of the road and walked the rest of the way.

When we entered the property we headed toward the Main Pond, expecting to see downed trees and limbs dangling precariously. But what we saw from a distance made us suddenly begin to run, as if getting there sooner would somehow soften the blow.

in the path of the flood, everything else was completely destroyed. We were stunned.

For the first two weeks after the storm, we couldn't sleep. We could not even imagine how we would ever be able to start this work over again. Ten years is such a long time to re-invent. At the beginning of each year, we had always felt that we had to give the garden new life. But we had had the previous years' work to build on. The task now at hand seemed impossible.

Shanti Bithi crews began cleaning up the mess and debris as we tried to regain our balance. Their intensity

Our beautiful gardens were obliterated! Ten years of work and obsessive creative energy had been destroyed by a torrent of muddy water that had picked up everything in its path, including the neighbor's fence from across the road, almost half a mile upstream.

Neither of us said a word. We saw everything else in slow motion. Wherever we looked, the devastation was unimaginable! We walked across what was left of the Grass Garden to inspect the Main Pond. When we reached the west side of the pond, above the Fern Garden, we saw that the fern hillside was completely gone (photo above). Hundreds and hundreds of yards of soil and thousands of plants had washed away. The terrace landing (see page 52) was destroyed, and a specimen *Acer palmatum* 'Seiryu' was floating in what was left of the Fern Garden Pond. The island in this pond had vanished, along with all the trees we had planted on it.

The stream bed entering the Main Pond was filled with tons of silt and gravel that had washed down from Croton Lake Road. We were afraid to enter the Duck Preserve, and with good reason: the entire netting had collapsed. Most of the ducks seemed to have escaped, but a few unfortunate ones had gotten tangled in the netting and drowned. All the beautiful plantings were gone. It was heartbreaking.

We had recently begun to feel that our work on the north side of the property, which included the Main Pond, the Maple Garden, the Fern Garden, and the Duck Preserve, was almost completed. Now, except for the Maple Garden, which was not

Devastation in the Duck Preserve

gave us new inspiration. The autumn days were becoming crisp, our winter holiday was approaching, and we felt ashamed to be thinking of giving up. Gradually my husband began imagining new gardens that might be as exquisite as those that had been washed away by Hurricane Floyd.

The Steinhardts hoped the Duck Preserve would one day be rebuilt, as well as all the other gardens that had been ruined. The most difficult challenge of all would be rebuilding the Preserve. While I felt overwhelmed by the commitment we were about to make, Gangadhar could sense new opportunities for his creativity. He began to envision a sanctuary even more beautiful than "duck heaven."

CHAPTER 25

AGAINST THE LAW

Facing page: The Duck Preserve

In January 2002 Gangadhar and I made a short visit to Brunei with our meditation group. As on most of our exotic trips, the first thing we did when we arrived was look for a stadium or track where we could do our workouts. We found an excellent one right next door to our hotel.

Brunei boasts one of the most luxurious hotels in the world—where we were, unfortunately, not staying. But we managed to eat all of our lunches and dinners there, so from my perspective this was a great trip. It was also a very short trip, and when we returned to the U.S. we were exhausted from jet lag.

Our flight home stopped in San Francisco. We spent one night at our son Narendra's apartment in Palo Alto, and flew to Portland the following morning. We had decided to make our annual buying trip to Oregon and Washington State right away, so that we could go down to San Diego for what was left of the winter, and stay put.

Our plan was to find a small motel near the first nursery we intended to visit, since we would be arriving too late to do any business that day. We felt that if we got an early start the following morning, we could finish our business in Oregon in one day and leave for Washington State, our next stop.

In Oregon, we knew where the nurseries were; but finding a motel was an entirely different matter. Exhausted, we drove around for more than an hour looking for something acceptable, and found nothing. "Gangadhar, just ask someone!" I said, exasperated. "You don't know where you're going."

That comment did not trigger a positive response from my husband. He abruptly exited the parkway, and I knew he was up to no good. "Just leave me alone," he mumbled. "I know what I'm doing."

Well, after 35-plus years of marriage, I also knew what he was doing. He was about to make a U-turn on a four-lane road to get back onto the parkway in the other direction. It was rush hour, and I was horrified. "Do not make a U-turn," I warned him. "It is against the law, and it's dangerous! You will get a huge ticket!"

But there was no stopping him. I could see how delighted he was with the way he skillfully maneuvered the car while making his turn. "You are breaking the law, and I hope you get stopped!" I shouted. "I hope you get a big ticket—with points! You deserve it!"

Within moments, the sirens began to wail, and we were pulled over by a trooper. Instead of being upset that he was about to get a summons, Gangadhar started yelling at me in front of the officer. "Are you happy? Are you satisfied? This is just what you wanted!"

Meanwhile, the officer waited politely outside the car window, unable to get a word in. When he was finally able to ask Gangadhar for his license and registration, we fumbled for the rental papers. Gangadhar began to make up a lame excuse explaining why he had made the U-turn. I was so furious that I leaned over and said, "*Give* him the ticket! He deserves it. I told him not to make that U-turn. He never listens to me!"

Expressionless, the officer took Gangadhar's license and registration and returned to his vehicle, while we continued to have it out.

When he came back, summons book in hand, he said, "In 99% of the cases, when I stop someone, I give them a ticket. Your license is clean, and I also happen to have a wife who I am going home to. I'm not going to ticket you, even though you did something illegal and very dangerous, because I can see that your wife will never let you hear the end of it."

Believe it or not, on one other occasion I begged an officer to give my husband a ticket, when he made a right turn on red, which is against the law in New York City. That officer also took pity on Gangadhar, and let him off.

Sequoiadendrum giganteum 'Pendulum' at Buchholz Nursery in Oregon

CHAPTER 26

ARCHITECTURAL INDIGESTION

The construction of many new buildings at the Steinhardts' had brought a lot of extra traffic onto the property. To solve the problem of all the comings and goings, Judy asked us to design a new main entrance. The existing entrance, at the top of a gracefully curving drive, had a unique and lovely wrought iron gate that had been imported from France several years earlier (see pages 88-89). The only way to make the proposed new entrance more important than the existing one, was to design an even more magnificent gate. We chose the theme of a Japanese maple.

We called upon our longtime collaborator Serge Bachelier, as we had done for many of the other gates on this property. Our specifications were that the gate had to be light and airy, yet strong enough to withstand the stresses of repeated opening and closing. And we did not want the tree to be enclosed within a frame. This, we felt, would make the gate both beautiful and unique.

The new Maple Gate arrived in May of 2002, meticulously protected in a wooden crate that Serge himself had built for the transport. For many days we left the gate in the opened crate, afraid to damage it while removing it. We would periodically stop by to admire it the way one goes to see new puppies.

A week before the scheduled June photo shoot for an upcoming article in *Architectural Digest,* Judy reminded us that she wanted the new gate installed before the photographer came. There was no more time for stalling. We carefully uncrated and installed the gate in the new main entrance to the property. It was spectacular. We thought it looked like the Gate to Eden.

When landscape photographer Scott Frances came to take pictures of the buildings and property for the upcoming article, he seemed captivated by this extraordinary gate. We secretly enjoyed watching how much time he spent photographing it. Gangadhar laughed about this, thinking maybe the new front entrance would even be on the cover of the magazine.

The following spring Shanti Bithi was asked to provide detailed written descriptions of our work on the property, including all the plantings we had done around the new buildings. *Architectural Digest* sent us nine photographs, requesting that we identify design objectives and plantings in each one. We spent days preparing a thorough documentation to give to the writer. For the Maple

The new Main Entrance

Gate, which was one of the nine photos, we included details of our collaboration with Serge Bachelier. We were so excited about the prospect of seeing our garden designs and plantings in *Architectural Digest*.

But when the article finally came out in the June 2003 issue, Shanti Bithi was not mentioned, Jerome Rocherolle was not mentioned, Serge Bachelier was not mentioned, and somehow, the architects' names appeared beneath a beautiful photo of the Maple Gate. Much to our dismay, the architects appeared to be given credit for everything on the property.

Our omission from the AD article was a huge disappointment. I obsessed for days about how this could have happened. It was one of many times I wished my mother were still alive. She was a great sympathizer, and could get all riled up when someone did her children wrong. But at the same time, my mom probably would have concluded, *"Abi gezunt."* (As long as you're healthy.) In other words: Be grateful for what you have. She always reminded me about what was really important in life.

In the fall of that year we had the good fortune to have our work featured in *AD Germany*, *Garden Design*, *House Beautiful*, *Vogue Country Living Australia* and *The New York Times*. *House & Garden* magazine began a photo shoot in 2004 for an upcoming feature, published in March, 2006.

Photos this page and previous page: The body of the Maple tree is hand-forged, as are a bird, a squirrel, and a tiny snail that adorn the branches. The tree has 248 individually cut maple leaves that were hand-struck approximately 52,000 times to achieve the serrations typical of Japanese maple leaves.

Uncrating the newest gate for the Aviary (see page 142)

CHAPTER 27

SWIMMING THE CHANNEL

My husband has done something truly astonishing—he has run a minimum of two miles every single day for the past 29 years. In spite of occasional fevers, a broken toe, a tooth abscess, and the normal array of running injuries, he has never missed a single day. Our entire family did a one year running streak together when the boys were in high school. And Gangadhar claims that I have run most of the days with him. But as much as he appreciates me for accompanying him on many of his runs, he is the one who has never missed, not once, for anything.

In the course of accomplishing this feat he has had some adventures. On one trip home from the Far East, Gangadhar's series of connecting flights meant he was in various airports for almost 36 hours. In Tokyo he had three hours between flights, so he decided to do his run around the perimeter of Narita Airport. The Japanese were strict about access to the airports even before 9/11. When the airport authorities spotted him, they took him to the police station. He was able to convince them that he had no bad intentions, and they released him in time to make his plane. Luckily, he had already completed his two miles before he was picked up.

He did only one of his runs indoors. That was in the Singapore airport, which is quite large, and he managed to run two miles in the long airport corridors. Meanwhile, during his streak, my husband ran more than 20 marathons—his best in

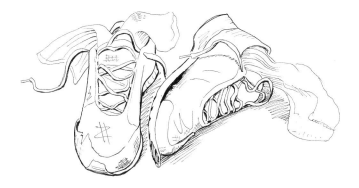

3:10 at age 40. He now runs middle distance on the track.

Along the way, Gangadhar was also inspired to swim the English Channel. He trained for two years, but always had difficulty finding places to do the long practice swims in cold water. His favorite training place was the Stamford Reservoir, where swimming happens to be prohibited. He would jog to the gate where he could access the reservoir, because he did not want his car to be spotted by anyone from the Stamford Water Company.

One morning Gangadhar was behind schedule and decided to drive to the reservoir instead of jogging over. Although he parked a discreet distance from the entrance that day, and managed to complete his swim, it took him a long time to find the running shoes that he had left by the water's edge. Finally, he heard a voice inquiring, "Are you looking for these?" It was a Stamford Water Company official holding up his shoes.

The official not only reprimanded him, but also issued a summons for trespassing, which required an appearance in court. Fortunately, the judge was impressed that my husband was practicing to swim the English Channel, and did not fine him. But Gangadhar had to promise to find another place to do his long swims.

After this experience, he began training in the Stamford Cove. One day, after a two-mile run on the beach, he left his brand new running shoes on the sand while he swam for an hour. When my husband came out of the water, once again his shoes were missing—but not for long. He soon spotted his new shoes on the feet of a local vagrant. This time he did not get them back.

Gangadhar left for Dover in late July to prepare for his attempt to swim the Channel. He was part of a group of Sri Chinmoy students who were also planning to do the swim. However, instead of going directly to England to practice with his friends, he went to La Rocherolle for ten days. There he swam in *le lavoir*, a spring-fed canal that had icy cold water, but was shallow and only 60 meters long (photo facing page). While he was able to gain a few needed pounds from eating Granny's delicious French cuisine, he probably should have stayed with the rest of the swimmers. The turbulent, filthy waters of Dover bore no resemblance to the tiny *lavoir* at La Rocherolle.

I had decided not to be in the boat when my husband made his crossing. It was less because I was needed at home to supervise our crews, and more because I did not think I would be very helpful. I was sure that if Gangadhar were to show any signs of distress or fatigue I would immediately insist that he come out of the water at once. I was not the right person to encourage him to keep going if I saw that he was suffering.

Even so, I began to feel a little guilty about not being there when he was trying something so momentous. My girlfriend Snigdha, who worked for Trans World Airlines (TWA), said she would accompany me if I decided to go. She had a free pass, so only one last-minute ticket had to be purchased. Snighda is the perfect person to go anywhere with. She was my former marathon training partner, and is a great storyteller.

Snigdha and I went to JFK Airport together. When we were about to get on the plane, she handed me her First Class boarding pass and whispered, "Try it, Gayatri, you'll *love* it." I know she did this out of the goodness of her heart, but for me it turned out to be very stressful. Despite the luxury of a fully reclining seat, I lay awake the whole night, worried that I would forget that my name was now Helene Fitch, which was how Snigdha's name appeared on the boarding pass and in the airplane manifest. Moreover, I was sure that somewhere it must have indicated that I worked for TWA, as this First Class pass was a company upgrade. I could not relax for even one minute.

Snigdha, on the other hand, was as cool as a cucumber. She was Carole Rocherolle, except for one mistake. Her hand luggage was a TWA company bag, which all the flight attendants recognize as a sign that you are an airline employee. The flight attendant, noticing her bag, went over to chat, just as I feared they would do with me. She asked Snigdha, "What are you doing back here? You should be in First Class."

Snigdha replied, without even a blink, "Oh, that's okay. I like it better back here in coach." Fortunately, we were not discovered.

Snigdha and I arrived in London, took a train to Dover, and went straight to Gangadhar's hotel. Much to our surprise, the front desk told us that my husband was in his room.

Thinking he might be resting after his workout, I quietly let myself in. Gangadhar was a sorry sight! Lying on his bed, still covered with a thick layer of white grease that he had applied for protection from the icy water, he was shivering uncontrollably from hypothermia. He had not been able to gain enough weight to keep his body temperature up, and had only lasted $2\frac{1}{2}$ hours in the icy waters of the English Channel.

I was relieved that I had decided to come after all. Snigdha and I warmed Gangadhar up with cups of hot soup, and moved him out of his tiny room and into a nicer hotel. The next morning we all left for home.

Poor Gangadhar was so disappointed. They didn't even allow him to attempt the Channel, because he had been unable to complete the required 5-hour practice swim. Fortunately, we had Snigdha to cheer us up. She kept us laughing with stories about her job in the TWA main ticket office in New York City—all the First Class upgrades she had given away to people with hard luck stories, and all the people she hadn't charged to change their tickets, because she felt sorry for them.

Tree Yuccas flowering in front of "The Ritz for Ring-tailed Lemurs"

CHAPTER 28
GARDENING ON THE EDGE

When we returned from Dover, we vowed to focus more of our attention on developing the plant collections. Gangadhar put the exhausting channel-swimming workouts on hold, and we began testing the limits of growing in climate zone 6.

For many years Shadow Nursery in Winchester, Tennessee, has been a great source of unusual plant material. My husband and I make regular visits to this nursery. One year Judy and Michael accompanied us. On that trip we selected several *Lagerstroemia* 'Tuskegee' (Crape

Don Shadow showing our horticulturist, Myron Porto, a variegated sport on the *Styrax obassia* growing at the lodge. Cuttings were taken to propagate.

myrtle) and planted a grouping at the entrance to the new Aviary (photo and inset below).

Anxious for these beautiful specimens to survive, we went to unprecedented lengths to winterize them. Gangadhar purchased pipe insulation at Home Depot, and we used it to wrap the trunks of the trees as high as ten feet. We also piled leaves $2\frac{1}{2}$ feet deep at the base of each tree. They all survived a harsh winter and continued to thrive.

The following year we protected them the Japanese way—with straw wrapped around each trunk. After the third winter, which was exceptionally cold, the grove appeared to have suffered. Gangadhar eliminated one tree, certain it had died. But to our surprise and delight, the others survived and flowered profusely. It is truly unusual to find Crape myrtle flowering in zone 6 on 25-foot trees.

We have tried several times to grow hardy Camellias. They made it through the first winter, but did not do well the second. This year we are experimenting with a new way to protect them. We have constructed

insulated "teepees" around each one (photos this page).

We winterize our entire collection of *Acer palmatum* by wrapping the trunks and major branches with burlap (photos this page). This is a time-consuming process, with almost 400 cultivars to wrap.

Last year Don Shadow sent us some tree Yuccas, which we planted in front of the new Lemur habitat, with little hope that they would overwinter. But they flowered beautifully, and continue to look strong and healthy (photo page 140).

We have one more fall ritual in addition to winterizing our thousands of plants: we build scarecrows. Every other year the Steinhardts host a Cider Party for several hundred of their friends. Decorating for this event is one of our favorite projects (photos on next 3 pages).

Marginally-hardy plants painstakingly wrapped for winter protection

CHAPTER 29

OUT OF THE BLOCKS

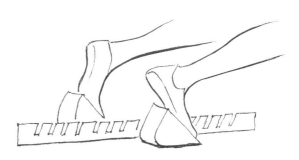

When my brother-in-law Michel saw what I was wearing to his daughter Sylvie's wedding, he came out into the courtyard in his matching undershorts and had this photo taken by the wedding photographer.

Granny and Bon Pappy had always encouraged us to spend our summer holidays at La Rocherolle, for as long as I can remember. In July of 1977, we were thirty-five in the castle. My in-laws prepared for weeks. "*On va être très nombreux cet été*," they used to say, when the *château* was going to be full. They prided themselves on having enough beds and sheets for everyone. The only other time the castle was filled to capacity was for weddings—and later, sadly, for funerals.

Gangadhar and I added to the numbers by inviting friends of ours from Switzerland and France to join us for a long weekend at the castle. Our friends were students of Sri Chinmoy, and we had a wonderful weekend of tennis, running and, of course, meditation. It was an odd combination: all of the Rocherolles

and "*les Sri Chinmoys*," as my brother-in-law Michel, a great joker, used to call them.

Well, while all of the Rocherolles were getting fat on the huge meals that lasted for hours, "*les Sri Chinmoys*" were going to the track and tennis courts in Argenton-sur-Creuse doing sports and more sports. In our meditation group, sports had become one of the main activities.

Soon after I returned from France that summer, a friend of mine asked if I would run the last few miles of the New York City Marathon with her. To this day, Nishtha credits me with inspiring her to run a sub 4-hour marathon, but the amount of support I was able to give her is questionable. I think she was helping me more than I was helping her. I ran the last seven miles of the marathon with her. It was the farthest, and definitely the fastest, I had ever run.

The following year I completed my first New York City Marathon in a time of 4:24. By May of the next year I had gone under 4 hours in the Long Island Marathon. I have run a total of 20 marathons, and nine of them were in New York City. Every marathon is memorable for one reason or another, but some stand out more than others.

One year my younger son volunteered to help by running the first few miles with me. I lost sight of him near the 6-mile mark, as he danced up the hill to the rhythmic music of a loud band playing for the runners. My concern for Durdam's whereabouts distracted me from my own discomfort. I got to the finish line that year much faster than I had anticipated. And my sixteen-year-old "helper" completed his first-ever marathon that day. He had never run farther than 4 miles before.

Durdam continues to play a pivotal role in my athletic career. In 1990 I broke my ankle. This meant I was out of commission for six weeks in a walking hard cast, and six more in a soft cast. I had never broken a bone before, and I had no idea what was awaiting me when the cast was removed: a limp, useless left leg.

My son was living in San Diego by that time, and training for the decathlon. He had a wonderful coach, Jarek Gwozdz, who himself had been a world-class high jumper. Durdam asked Jarek to give me exercises to rehabilitate my leg. A new chapter in my life began like that, with simple strengthening exercises. My rehabilitation was quick.

Months later, when Jarek and Durdam came to New York for a competition, I invited my friend Lavanya to come to the track with me. Jarek surprised us by asking us to run a 60-meter time trial. We reluctantly agreed, never imagining what this

© 2005 Teri Cluck

Coach Durdam with Angel

would lead to. Neither of us had any background in track and field—we were distance runners. But both of us had discipline and determination. With Jarek's and Durdam's coaching, we improved rapidly and soon began entering age-group competitions in the 100 and 200 meter events.

The World Veterans Games were to be held in Miyazaki, Japan, the following year. Durdam signed us up without even asking. Knowing how much we loved Japan, he figured

we would be delighted to have a good reason to go there. He was right; we reserved our plane tickets immediately.

To prepare us for the competition, our two coaches ratcheted up our training regimen. Durdam even convinced his father to enter the meet, despite the fact that we were over-committed at work.

Miyazaki was an unforgettable experience for all of us. The meet included 12,000 participants from more than 78 countries. Most of these athletes were former national champions and even Olympic medalists. When Durdam accompanied us to pick up our numbers, he sheepishly admitted that he had seriously underestimated the level of competition his athletes (us!) would be facing.

The many events of the Miyazaki Masters Games were staged on two different tracks simultaneously, and a third track was available for warm-ups. The Japanese organizers had done their best to re-create an Olympic ambience. Check-in for an event was two hours prior to starting time, and just like in the Olympics, we were led onto the track in the order of our lane assignments. And here is the worst part: When your heat was announced, your name and country went up on the board in lights. It's not as if you were nameless, and people could wonder, "Who is that person in lane 6?" No such luck. Miyazaki was the big time.

Oh my God! It was the most terrifying experience I could ever imagine. Before my first event, the 200m, I thought I would not even be able to get into the blocks. I had

had no previous experience with the rituals of calming myself down in such an intimidating setting. I consider it my biggest triumph to this day that when the gun went off, I went out of the blocks and ran my best time ever (photo below).

My track workouts are an integral part of my spiritual life. Sprinting is my metaphor. When you go out of the blocks, you are giving 100% of yourself. Right from the start, you have no thoughts – you only listen for the gun. There is no holding back.

Sri Chinmoy gave me instructions on how to go out of the starting blocks. He taught me to keep my arms straight, as close to my knees as possible, to hold my head down, relaxed, and to lean forward with my shoulders. He is an excellent coach. His enthusiasm and love of sports have been my true inspiration.

Lavanya and I nervously await our first event.

"Runners to your mark..." – I'm in lane 6.

Coming off the turn in the 200 meters

第10回世界ベテランズ陸上競技選手権大会　　平成5年10月7日～17日　宮崎市にて。

CHAPTER 30
SMALL ANIMAL HABITATS

When six Ring-tailed Lemurs came to live on the Stein-hardt estate, neither my husband nor I had ever heard of these animals. But this addition to Michael's fast-growing collection meant that once again new habitats had to be created. After obsessively down-loading page after page of documents detailing Lemur behavior, diet, environment, and reproductive habits, we were off and running, visiting zoos.

We went first to the San Francisco Zoo, which had just completed the most extensive Lemur exhibit in the country. The installation looked like the backyard swing-and-slide sets that are popping up like mushrooms across the country, but ten times bigger. None of the U.S. zoos had anything that we found useful from a design perspective, but in our travels we learned a great deal about the needs of these adorable animals.

It wasn't until we visited New Zealand in 2002 with our meditation center, that we found inspiration for a habitat concept. The New Zealand zoos were often as beautifully designed and landscaped as the botanical gardens there, for which the country is famous. Animal preserves in New Zealand do not have the resources of American zoos. Their designers are forced to be more creative in the simplest of ways. One particular zoo outside Christchurch on the South Island had designed wonderfully inventive habitats—just the kind of thing we were looking for.

Shortly before going on this trip we had begun work on a new pond in the west paddock facing the site that had been chosen for the Lemur habitat. The day we set down the

Area enclosed by netting for visitors   Interior View from doors (in area enclosed by netting)

Conceptual drawings both pages by
Edward Henrey

liner for this pond was one of the happiest days we have ever spent in our landscape life. It took every one of Shanti Bithi's *hermanos y primos* (brothers and cousins) to carry this enormous pond liner across the paddock. The sight of these men, proudly marching to the pond bearing the heavy liner on their shoulders, brought tears to my eyes.

The liner was so big that it had to be shipped in two separate pieces. Once we had set both sections in place, we had to glue the giant seam. Although the late autumn afternoon had been warm, the temperature was dropping rapidly. The glue would not take at less than forty degrees. We worked into the early evening, anxiously watching the thermometer. Fortunately, the glue held and we were able to fill the pond before the first early December snowstorm only days later.

Building the Lemur Pavillion was our next project. (Early design concepts appear on the previous two pages.) The building itself took a year to complete, and it is so luxurious that we refer to it as "The Ritz for Ring-tailed Lemurs" (photos pages 140 and next page bottom). Naturally curious and acrobatic, the Lemurs, with their long striped tails, big dark eyes, and dainty paws, are the most popular animals on the property. Judy and Michael love bringing their guests to feed and admire them.

Not long after the Lemur Pavilion was completed, Gangadhar began designing a porcupine cave. The African Porcupines are the most destructive animals on the estate.

They can gnaw through heavy-gauge wire in one night. To house these aggressive animals, we designed a habitat with a stone fence and a cement floor. Primarily nocturnal, the porcupines spend most of the daytime inside the stone caves we constructed to protect them from too much sunlight.

For the six colorful Macaws we designed an outdoor enclosure near the barns, under a canopy of Osage Orange and *Cratageus* (photo right). During the summer months these exotic birds enjoy the freedom of their spacious outdoor habitat. When the weather gets cooler, they are cared for in the heated barns.

Our next project is a home for the Caracal cats. We are designing a habitat that will give them as much open space as possible for jumping and climbing.

Since the animals in the Steinhardt collection are always producing offspring, we have learned to anticipate the baby boom. My husband enjoys the challenge of designing these small animal habitats and integrating them into their surroundings as seamlessly as possible.

Feeding grapes to the Lemurs

Poorly attired for a muddy construction site . . .

CHAPTER 31
FOOTSTEPS

In 1986, when Narendra was accepted at Princeton, I became totally undone. Many of my friends and family still had young children at home, and I was so envious of them. One morning I actually drove to my son's old nursery school and sat in the parking lot crying as I watched other parents dropping off their toddlers. I even poured my heart out to my old friend Mona, now Dr. Mona Ackerman, a psychologist. "It's so far away, Mona. I won't even be able to do his laundry!"

"Carrie," she said, "I love you, honey, but you're insane!" Now, that gave me pause.

Two years later, life taught me another lesson in letting go. Durdam, my baby, moved to San Diego right after graduating from high school. Instead of remaining on the east coast for four more years as I had hoped, he became a California state resident, convinced his grandmother to give him the money she had allocated for tuition at a private university, and enrolled at San Diego State, a Division One school.

Durdam was intent on becoming a decathlete, and that is exactly what he did. Within one year he was competing in the grueling two-day event, and he was one of the first Americans to compete in the one-hour decathlon—all ten events in one hour.

When Narendra, also a track aficionado, graduated from Princeton, he moved to California to live and train with his brother. My mother, who had had a similar experience to mine when my brother, Jon, moved to the west coast, tried to console me. "Don't worry, sweetheart. They'll be fine as long as they are together."

In a way, that was my assurance that I, too, was going to be fine,

even with both my boys so far away. And I was, of course, though I admit I helped things along by flying out to California as often as I could.

My mother was right about the boys doing well together. Together they began one of the first fifty internet design/consulting companies in the world. Webspin Technologies was how they incorporated.

Finding customers was not an easy task in 1994, as almost no one in San Diego had even heard about the internet. But Gangadhar and I were not alarmed. We were firm believers in the entrepreneurial spirit, and were excited that our boys had chosen to begin their own enterprise.

Webspin was one of the first customers for Broadcast.com, the company Mark Cuban and his partners began in Texas. In 1998 Narendra was hired by Andy Laakmann, who had been one of Webspin's first clients. Andy, Narendra, and Nick Wilder, a computer engineer, became founding partners of Webshots, and the three of them grew their company into a popular photo-sharing site.

The dot-com era was booming, but Andy sensed that there was only a small window of opportunity to sell their company. After only three months of marketing it, they had a buyer. Webshots was sold to Excite@Home for a huge sum, mostly in stock, which had to vest over time. It was a "reverse triangular merger" and a good deal for the young entrepreneurs.

Although Excite@Home went bankrupt two years later (it was one of the first large tech companies to suffer this fate), good fortune followed the Webshots founders. Durdam encouraged his brother to buy back Webshots out of bankruptcy court, and he himself became a minority shareholder when the purchase was completed.

Nick and Narendra were now at the helm of Webshots (Andy had retired) and they hired some of the best talent from the bankrupt Excite. They hit the jackpot when they were able to hire Julie Davidson. She became a partner and the company's COO and CFO.

Webshots was cash positive after just 90 days, and within two years it had grown into the largest photo-sharing site in the world.

All of us at Durdam's house in La Jolla, 1995

Then they did it again. Narendra and his partners sold their company once again, this time to the online technology news provider, CNET.

But to me, the mom, the best part of the deal is that the former COO/CFO of Webshots has now become Mrs. Narendra Rocherolle.

My childrens' growing and changing lives, even at a distance, continue to enrich mine. They are, and will always remain, my purest source of joy and satisfaction.

Julie at La Rocherolle—her first visit

CHAPTER 32
CONCLUSION

In 2002 our winter holiday with the meditation center took us to New Zealand. We enjoyed this trip so much that we almost didn't want to come home. Our month-long stay inspired and renewed us. The clean air, like the air we used to breathe when we were young, and the pure mountain streams, made us realize that no manmade garden can come close to the pristine beauty of an untouched world.

Our visits to the botanical gardens in New Zealand confirmed to us how knowledgeable we had become in horticulture. We knew and recognized most of the plants, and we have utilized many of them in our own garden designs.

What truly amazed us was that the Steinhardt Gardens compared favorably to even the most re-nowned gardens we visited in this horticultural paradise. In fact, we felt that the Steinhardt Gardens were more beautiful than any we saw there, because our goal has always been to naturalize the plant collections, making the aesthetics as important as the plant material.

Having the opportunity to design and build a private botanical-like garden has been a tremendous boon for our professional life. But we cannot claim the beautiful gardens that we have created as our legacy. Even before our lives move on from this big job that we give so much importance to, there will be many more lessons of humility to learn.

The breathtaking panoramas of the New Zealand countryside humbled us and made us realize that it was the high standard we always tried to maintain while we did our work that would give us abiding satisfaction in the years to come. Not what we did, but how we did it.

The gardens we build are like sand castles. We can fashion them and watch them grow, but no matter what we do to preserve and protect them, nature will surely have the last word.

EPILOGUE

We brought Granny back to France to be buried, just as we had done for Bon Pappy. She had lived for five years, almost to the day, without her husband of 62 years. Her body remained in the chapel at La Rocherolle for several days, while friends and family came to pay their last respects.

We had a private service, when each of us said goodbye to her in our own way, as we had done for Gangadhar's father. And then *les petits fils* (the grandsons) lifted her coffin into the black station wagon that took her to Tendu, a small village only two miles up the hill from the *château*. The Catholic Mass was just like the one we had had for Bon Pappy, with the same outside priest. The tiny church in Tendu is too poor and unimportant to have its own priest any longer.

Granny was laid to rest in the local cemetery, so close to the church that we all walked there behind the casket. It was early November, but it was a beautiful, sunny, almost warm day. After the Mass we served lunch at La Rocherolle for the hundred or so friends and family who had come.

It was a tearful day, but also a happy day because we were all together.

That afternoon Durdam's best friends, Steve and Amy Finley, arrived from California. It was their first trip to France. Although it was an unlikely weekend to have guests, we knew Granny would have been happy that they had come. Welcoming friends—and friends of friends, even at distant removes—was a tradition she and Bon Pappy had begun. Hospitality was their legacy.

The following day we took Amy and Steve to Gargilesse to meet Serge Bachelier. He was not working on anything for us at the time, but we wanted them to meet him and see the beautiful view of the *Vallée de la Creuse* from his workshop.

We ran out of gas en route. I had reminded Gangadhar to gas up before the weekend, but to no avail. We sputtered into the driveway of a local resident and begged him to siphon gas from his own tank so that we could make it the rest of the way to Gargilesse and back home.

Even with the joy of hosting friends who had never been there before, I secretly planned to wait a long time before returning to La Rocherolle. I felt it would be too painful to come and not have any parents there to receive us.

We did not return until the summer of our 35th wedding anniversary. Narendra and Durdam invited a group of their friends for a long weekend at the castle to celebrate with us. Gangadhar and I arrived at La Rocherolle only hours ahead of the ten guests we were expecting, and began shopping madly to fill the house with enough food to provide the enormous feasts that one comes to expect on a visit to this castle.

The weather was warm. It was July, and the days were long. We ate all our meals outside in the courtyard. During lunch on the day before we were to leave for home, I noticed that my husband was preoccupied. He was staring at the large *Taxus* (Yew), which had spread so wide over the years that much of the courtyard was now covered by its dark green drooping branches. He had his eye on this great tree, and I knew something was up.

After lunch our boys and their friends left for Val d'Isère to go mountain climbing. Their departure meant that my husband and I now had the castle to ourselves for the first time in all these years.

Gangadhar went into town that very afternoon and purchased a hand saw to begin the giant task of pruning up the branches of the tree he had been eyeing. This was an idea he had mentioned to Bon Pappy many years earlier. But his suggestion that he prune this 400-year-old tree had been met with such disapproval that he did not bring up the subject a second time. Now there was no Bon Pappy and no Granny. So Gangadhar dared to begin pruning this enormous tree.

At first I thought he would clean up only the bottom branches, and he started by doing just that. I hoped Gangadhar would be satisfied then, and return on another occasion to complete the job. But it soon became evident that he had no plans to stop pruning, even when it was past dinnertime.

He got out the rickety old ladder, climbed to the top of it, and continued pruning as far as his arms could reach. A heavy branch he was taking down fell suddenly and cut his face. Gangadhar came down off the ladder covered with blood. I begged him to call it a day, but it was no use. He continued sawing away at this tree that he felt was blocking the entrance to the Chapel and taking up too much space in the courtyard, where we all spent most of our time when the weather was nice.

We had to leave early the next morning in order to make our plane, so while Gangadhar pruned, I dragged all the heavy branches out into the service driveway and set them in neat piles. We didn't want to leave the courtyard filled with debris, because our niece Annick was arriving the following morning with her family.

Gangadhar did not finish his work until almost midnight. Exhausted, we both sat down on the living room couch in front of the large empty fireplace. At this point we were almost too tired to go up the two flights of stairs to our bedroom for a short night's sleep. But something else made both of us linger even longer downstairs.

It was the silence. There was no one else in the castle—no parents, no children, no sisters and brothers, no nieces and nephews. We were going to leave early in the morning, and there was no one to say goodbye to. There would be no one at the door of the kitchen, waving to us and hurrying back into the castle to plan for the next meal or the next guests who might be arriving almost as we left.

It was a sad, quiet moment. We were now the parents left behind. We both felt deeply the silence and the ache in our hearts for our own parents, who would have cared that we were leaving, and who would have been so happy that we had come.

It was 35 years since our honeymoon in Corsica and my first visit, when the castle was gloomy and Bonne Maman was dressed all in black. I don't think we had ever shared a more poignant moment. I looked at Gangadhar. The cut under his eye was swollen after his overly ambitious tree-pruning, but he was still so handsome, and his smile so sweet. I had really married my prince. I felt incredibly blessed for the life we had shared, and especially for our boys. We were great together, just as Lillian had promised.

Grateful Acknowledgments

To my husband – my fifty-fifty partner – and our children, Narendra, Durdam, and Julie . . .

To Lavanya, my editor and training partner, with love and gratitude for her endless hours of creative work . . .

To Mike Totilo, our friend and advisor . . .

To Shanti Bithi Nursery staff, workers, and associates during the past 36 years: Myron Porto (horticulturist), Saeko Oshiro (garden designer and Bonsai expert), Caroline Rocherolle (garden designer), Janet Winston, Harriet McManus, Didier Rocherolle, Meghna Brower, Pierre Marandon, Richard Gottfried, Papaha Gosline, Kevin Foley, Constantino Bastian, Daniel Colon, David Romero, Edras Cabrera, Eduardo Sebastian, Guillermo Hernandez, Hugo Sebastian, Javier Bastian, Juan Sebastian, Lino Sebastian Batallar, Luis Sebastian, Manuel Segura, Marcelino Diaz, Max Mojica, Omar Cruz, Oscar Sanchez, Oscar Sandoval, Pascual Escobar, Pedro Sebastian, Placido Sebastian, Rudi Sebastian, Saul Sebastian, Saul Folgar, Bernardo Batallar, Yolanda Juarez, John Guido, Tapas Capo, Kalpanantit Broderick, Adarini Inkei, Sevati Bondanza, Allison Grossman, Mace Picken, Abedan Solomon, the late Angel Sebastian . . .

To Pahar Hal Meltzer, Suniti Martha Keys, Vasudha Deming, and Catie Lazarus for their invaluable assistance and expertise . . .

To Susan Slack and Matthew Hyner at Ruder Finn Press . . .

To the Brooklyn Botanic Garden, the New York Botanical Garden, Dr. Kim Tripp, the Bartlett Arboretum, Don Shadow, Manny Shemin, Dr. Bill Conway, John Gwynne, Marco Polo Stufano, Wave Hill, Steve Scaniello, Mike Lubbock, Barry Yinger, John Skovrun, Paul Auteri, John Currie . . .

To Joe and Ida D'Addona, David Abelow, Andrew Ballard, Victoria Borus . . .

To Anne and Dick Solomon, Sue and Arthur Warshaw, Linda and Lenny Chazen, the late Michael Shure, the Cullman Family, the late Hedy Kravis, Linda and Stuart Feld, Sue 2 and Jimmy Knowles, Margaret and Charlie Bowen, Linda and Kyle Felt, Noriko Prince . . .

To my friends and family for their love: the late Sylvia Hayes, Durthy Perry, Flora Barber, and Lillian Poses, to Anne-Marie Doricent, Eloise Mathis, Roz Lazarus, Barbara and Jon Avnet, Ruth Brody, Catherine Lepoutre, Marie-Laure and Michel Epron, Bénédicte Epron, Akuti Eisaman, Jarek Gwozdz, Amy and Steve Finley, Mary and Joaquim Cruz, Dr. Mona Ackerman, Deborah Santana, Kitsaun King, Meshulam Riklis, Dr. Helena 'Boge' Jones, Jayme Stewart, Snigdha Fitch, Cathy Waterman, Meshulam Riklis, Dr. Edythe Heus, Suzy Marcus, Susie and Butch Miller, Tyagambar Ramos, Samarpita Broderick, Simon Lazarus III, Charles Brown, Elizabeth O'Regan, Angela Hurson . . .

And especially to my parents.

Source Guide

Mail-order suppliers

Antique Rose Emporium
    www.antiqueroseemporium.com
Asiatica Nursery
    www.asiaticanursery.com
Camellia Forest Nursery
    www.camforest.com
Carroll Gardens
    www.carrollgardens.com
Clematis Nursery
    www.clematisnursery.com
Edible Landscaping
    www.ediblelandscaping.com
Fairweather Gardens
    www.fairweathergardens.com
Foliage Gardens
    www.foliagegardens.com
Forest Farm
    www.forestfarm.com
Heronswood Nursery
    www.heronswood.com

Hortico Nurseries
    www.hortico.com
Joy Creek Nursery
    www.joycreek.com
K. van Bourgondien
    www.dutchbulbs.com
Klehm's Nursery
    www.klehm.com
Ladybug Daylilies
    www.ladybugdaylilies.com
Lilypons Water Garden
    www.lilypons.com
McClure & Zimmerman
    www.mzbulb.com
Miller Nurseries
    www.millernurseries.com
New England Bamboo Company
    www.newengbamboo.com
Niche Gardens
    www.nichegardens.com
Oakes Daylilies
    www.oakesdaylilies.com
One Green World (Northwood)
    www.onegreenworld.com
Plant Delights Nursery
    www.plantdelights.com
Raintree Nursery
    www.raintreenursery.com
Rare Find Nursery
    www.rarefindnursery.com
Select Plus Int'l Lilac Nursery (W)
    www.spi.8m.com
Shadow Nursery (W)
    (931) 967-6059
Siskiyou Rare Plant Nursery
    www.srpn.net
Swan Island Dahlias
    www.dahlias.com
Tranquil Lake Nursery
    www.tranquil-lake.com
Trees of Antiquity
    www.treesofantiquity.com
Van Engelen
    www.vanengelen.com
Variegated Foliage Nursery
    www.variegatedfoliage.com
Wayside Gardens
    www.waysidegardens.com

WeDu (Meadowbrook Nursery)
    www.we-du.com
White Flower Farm
    www.whiteflowerfarm.com
Woodlander's Inc.
    www.woodlanders.net

(W) = wholesale only

Local suppliers

Baier Lustgarten (W)
    (609) 758-7600
Bedford Stone
    www.bedfordstone.com
Beds and Borders (W)
    www.bedsandborders.com
Capacchione Greenhouses (W)
    (860) 887-8107
Carlson's Gardens
    www.carlsonsgardens.com
Casertano's Greenhouse (W)
    (203) 272-6444
Claire's Garden Center
    (845) 878-6632
Cricket Hill Garden
    www.treepeony.com
Designs by Lee
    (203) 322-2206
Elmwood Greenhouses
    (914) 949-2756
Environmentals (W)
    www.environmentalsnursery.com
Evergreen Nursery
    (914) 232-7771
Gilberties Herb Garden (W)
    www.gilbertiesherbs.com
Halka Nursery (W)
    (732) 462-8450
Hardscrabble Farms (W)
    (914) 669-5633
Lawton Adams
    www.lawtonadams.com
Marders of Bridgehampton
    www.marders.com
Martin Brooks Rare Plant Nursery
    www.rareplantnursery.com

Matterhorn Nursery
    www.matterhornnursery.com
McArdle's Nursery
    www.mcardles.com
McCue Gardens (W)
    (860) 529-0937
Nabel's Nurseries
    (914) 949-3963
Oliver Nurseries
    www.olivernurseries.com
Outhouse Orchards
    (914) 277-3188
Pinewood Perennial Nursery (W)
    (631) 734-6911
Pleasant Run Nursery (W)
    www.pleasantrunnursery.com
Pound Ridge Nursery
    www.prnurseries.com

Princeton Nurseries (W)
    www.princetonnurseries.com
Rosedale Nurseries
    www.rosedalenurseries.com
Roth Nursery (W)
    (914) 273-8399
Sam Bridge Nursery
    www.sambridge.com
Shemin Nursery (W)
    www.shemin.net
Skovrun Nursery
    (203) 531-7586
Summer Hill Nursery (W)
    www.summerhillnursery.com
Sunny Border Nurseries (W)
    www.sunnyborder.com
The Plant Group (W)
    www.theplantgroup.com

The Plantage (W)
    www.plantage.com
Troy's Garden Nurseries
    (914) 234-3400
Twombly Nursery
    www.twomblynursery.com
Valley View Greenhouse (W)
    www.wgh.com
Weston Nurseries
    www.westonnurseries.com
White Flower Farm
    www.whiteflowerfarm.com
Whitmores Tree Farms
    www.whitmoresinc.com
Young's Nurseries
    www.youngsnurseries.com

Red Bridge by Bow House

The Steinhardt Maple Collection

Acer japonicum 'Aconitifolium europea'
Acer palmatum 'Aekan le's'
Acer palmatum 'Aka shigitatsu sawa'
Acer palmatum 'Aka shime no uchi'
Acer palmatum 'Akegarasu'
Acer palmatum 'Akita yatsubusa'
Acer palmatum 'Alpenweiss'
Acer palmatum 'Amagi shigure'

Acer palmatum 'Ao kanzashi'
Acer palmatum 'Ao shidare'
Acer palmatum 'Ao shime no uchi'
Acer palamtum 'Aoba jo'
Acer palmatum 'Aocha nishiki'
Acer palmatum 'Aoyagi'
Acer palmatum 'Arakawa'
Acer palmatum 'Aratama'
Acer palmatum 'Ariadne'
Acer palmatum 'Ariake nomura'

Acer palmatum 'Asahi zuru'
Acer linearlobum 'Atrolineare'
Acer palmatum 'Atropurpureum'
Acer palmatum 'Attraction'
Acer palmatum 'Auegarasu'
Acer palmatum 'Aureum'
Acer shirasawanum 'Aureum'
Acer palmatum 'Autumn Fire'
Acer palmatum 'Azuma murasaki'

Acer palmatum 'Baby Lace'
Acer palmatum 'Baldsmith'
Acer palmatum 'Baltzar's'
Acer palmatum 'Bamboo Bark'
Acer palmatum 'Barrie Bergman'
Acer palmatum 'Beni fushigi'
Acer palmatum 'Beni gasa'
Acer palmatum 'Beni hime'
Acer palmatum 'Beni hoshi'
Acer palmatum 'Beni kagami'
Acer palmatum 'Beni kawa'
Acer palmatum 'Beni komachi'
Acer palmatum 'Beni komo no bu'
Acer palmatum 'Beni kumo-no-un'
Acer palmatum 'Beni maiko'
Acer palmatum 'Beni musume'
Acer palmatum 'Beni otake'
Acer palmatum 'Beni schichihenge'
Acer palmatum 'Beni shi en'
Acer palmatum 'Beni shidare'
Acer palmatum 'Beni tsukasa'
Acer palmatum 'Beni ubi gohan'
Acer palmatum 'Berrima Bridge'
Acer palmatum 'Berry Dwarf'
Acer palmatum 'Bob's Big Green'
Acer palmatum 'Bonnie Bergman'
Acer palmatum 'Boskoop Glory'
Acer palmatum 'Brandt's Dwarf'
Acer palmatum 'Brocade'
Acer palmatum 'Bronzewing'
Acer palmatum 'Burgundy Lace'
Acer palmatum 'Burning Bush'
Acer palmatum 'Burnt Orange'
Acer palmatum 'Butterfly'

Acer palmatum 'Calico'
Acer palmatum 'Caperci Dwarf'
Acer palmatum 'Chiba'
Acer palmatum 'Chishio Improved'
Acer palmatum 'Chitoseyama'
Acer palmatum 'Coonara Pygmy'
Acer palmatum 'Corallinum'
Acer palmatum 'Crimson Queen'
Acer palmatum 'Crispum'
Acer palmatum 'Cristatum
    Variegatum'
Acer palmatum 'Curtis Strapleaf'
Acer palmatum 'Cynthia's Crown
    Jewel'

Acer palmatum 'Diane Verkade'
Acer palmatum 'Dissectum Nigrum'
Acer palmatum 'Dreiser'

Acer palmatum 'Eagle's Claw'
Acer palmatum 'Ebony'
Acer palmatum 'Ed's Red'
Acer palmatum 'Elegans'
Acer palmatum 'Emerald Lace'
Acer palmatum 'Elmwoodie'
Acer palmatum 'Emperor One'
Acer palmatum 'Englishtown'
Acer palmatum 'Enkan'
Acer palmatum 'Ever Red'
Acer palmatum 'Ezo no o momigi'

Acer palmatum 'Fairy Hair'
Acer palmatum 'Fall's Fire'
Acer palmatum 'Fascination'
Acer palmatum 'Filifera purpurea'
Acer palmatum 'Filigree'
Acer palmatum 'Fireglow'
Acer palmatum 'First Ghost'
Acer palmatum 'Fjellheim'
Acer palmatum 'Flushing'

Acer palmatum 'Garnet'
Acer palmatum 'Geisha'

Acer palmatum 'Germaine's
    Gyration'
Acer palmatum 'Glowing Embers'
Acer palmatum 'Goshiki kotohime'
Acer palmatum 'Goshiki shidare'
Acer palmatum 'Green Cascade'
Acer palmatum 'Green Elf'
Acer palmatum 'Green Flag'
Acer palmatum 'Green Hornet'
Acer palmatum 'Green Mist'
Acer palmatum 'Green Seedling'
Acer palmatum 'Green Star'
Acer palmatum 'Green
    Trompenberg'

Acer palmatum 'Hagoromo'
Acer palmatum 'Hanami nishiki'
Acer palmatum 'Hanazono nishiki'
Acer palmatum 'Harusame'
Acer palmatum 'Hatsu shigare'
Acer palmatum 'Heptalobum'
Acer palmatum 'Herbstfeuer'
Acer palmatum 'Hessei'
Acer palmatum 'Higasa yama'
Acer palmatum 'Hillieri'
Acer palmatum 'Hogyoku'
Acer palmatum 'Hohman's
    Variegated'
Acer palmatum 'Hoshi kuzu'
Acer palmatum 'Hubb's Red Willow'
Acer palmatum 'Hupp's Dwarf'

Acer palmatum 'Ibo Nishiki'
Acer palmatum 'Ichigyoji'
Acer palmatum 'Iijima sunago'
Acer palmatum 'In the Pink'
Acer palmatum 'Inaba shidare'
Acer palmatum 'Inazuma'
Acer palmatum 'Irish Lace'
Acer palmatum 'Iro iro'
Acer palmatum 'Iso chidori'
Acer palmatum 'Issai nishiki'
Acer palmatum 'Itame nobula'
Acer palmatum 'Itami nibuki'

Acer palmatum 'Itami nishiki'
Acer palmatum 'Italy Red'

Acer palmatum 'J.B. 31'
Acer palmatum 'Japanese Sunrise'
Acer palmatum 'Jiro shidare'
Acer palmatum 'Johnnie's Pink'
Acer palmatum 'JJ'
Acer palmatum 'Julia'
Acer palmatum 'Junihitoye'

Acer palmatum 'Kagero'
Acer palmatum 'Kagiri nishiki'
Acer palmatum 'Kamagata'
Acer palmatum 'Kandy Kitchen'
Acer palmatum 'Karasu gawa'
Acer palmatum 'Kasagi yama'
Acer palmatum 'Kasen nishiki'
Acer palmatum 'Katsura'
Acer palmatum 'Keiser'
Acer palmatum 'Ki hachijo'
Acer palmatum 'Killarney'
Acer palmatum 'Kingsville
    Variegated'
Acer palmatum 'Kinran'
Acer palmatum 'Kinshi'

Acer palmatum 'Kiri nishiki'
Acer palmatum 'Kiyohime'
Acer palmatum 'Klaas Red'
Acer palmatum 'Kogane nishiki'
Acer palmatum 'Kogane sakae'
Acer palmatum 'Komachi hime'
Acer palmatum 'Komon nishiki'
Acer palmatum 'Koreanum'
Acer palmatum 'Korean Gem'
Acer palmatum 'Koshibori nishiki'
Acer palmatum 'Koshimino'
Acer palmatum 'Koto maru'
Acer palmatum 'Koto no ito'
Acer palmatum 'Kotohime'
Acer palmatum 'Kurabe yama'
Acer palmatum 'Kurui jishi'

Acer palmatum 'Lady's Choice'
Acer palmatum 'Lemon Chiffon'
Acer palmatum 'Lemon Lime Lace'
Acer palmatum 'Lionheart'
Acer palmatum 'Lovett'
Acer palmatum 'Lozita'
Acer palmatum 'Lutescens'

Acer palmatum 'Maiko'
Acer japonicum 'Maiku Jaku'
Acer palmatum 'Maimori'
Acer palmatum 'Mama'
Acer palmatum 'Marakumo'
Acer palmatum 'Margaret Bee'
Acer palmatum 'Masu kagami'
Acer palmatum 'Masu murasaki'
Acer palmatum 'Matsuekaze'
Acer palmatum 'Matsugae'
Acer palmatum 'Matsuyoi'
Acer palmatum 'Mejishi'
Acer palmatum 'Microphyllum'
Acer palmatum 'Midori no teiboku'
Acer palmatum 'Mikawa yatsabusa'
Acer palmatum 'Mikomo nishiki'
Acer palmatum 'Mini monde'
Acer palmatum 'Miyame'
Acer palmatum 'Mirte'

Acer palmatum 'Mizu kagiri'
Acer palmatum 'Mizuho beni'
Acer palmatum 'Momenshide'
Acer palmatum 'Momiji nishiki'
Acer palmatum 'Monzukushi'
Acer palmatum 'Monroe'
Acer palmatum 'Moonfire'
Acer palmatum 'Murasaki kiyohime'
Acer palmatum 'Mure hibari'
Acer palmatum 'Muro gawa'
Acer palmatum 'Musa kagami'
Acer palmatum 'Mushashino'

Acer palmatum 'Nanase gawa'
Acer palmatum 'Nicholsonii'
Acer palmatum 'Nishiki gawa'
Acer palmatum 'Nishiki momiji'
Acer palmatum 'Noburei'
Acer palmatum 'Nomura nishiki'
Acer palmatum 'Novum'
Acer palmatum 'Nurasagi'
Acer palmatum 'O isami'

Acer palmatum 'O kagami'
Acer palmatum 'Octopus'
Acer palmatum 'Ogino nagare'
Acer palmatum 'Ogon sarasa'
Acer palmatum 'Ogura yama'
Acer palmatum 'Ojishi'
Acer palmatum 'Okushimo'
Acer palmatum 'Omato'
Acer palmatum 'Omurayama'
Acer palmatum 'Orange Dream'
Acer palmatum 'Orangeola'
Acer palmatum 'Oregon Cascade'
Acer palmatum 'Oregon Fern'
Acer palmatum 'Oregon Sunset'
Acer palmatum 'Orido nishiki'
Acer palmatum 'Ornatum'
Accr palmatum 'Osakazuki'
Acer palmatum 'Oshio beni'
Acer palmatum 'Oshu shidare'
Acer palmatum 'Oto hime'
Acer palmatum 'Otome zakura'
Acer palmatum 'Otto's'

Acer palmatum 'Palmatifidium'
Acer palmatum 'Peaches & Cream'
Acer palmatum 'Pendulum
    Angustilobum Atropurpureum'
Acer palmatum 'Pendulum Julian'
Acer palmatum 'Pixie'
Acer palmatum 'Purple Ghost'

Acer palmatum 'Raraflora'
Acer palmatum 'Red Autumn Lace'
Acer palmatum 'Red Baron'
Acer palmatum 'Red Cloud'
Acer palmatum 'Red Crusader'
Acer palmatum 'Red Dragon'
Acer palmatum 'Red Feather'
Acer palmatum 'Red Filigree Lace'
Acer palmatum 'Red Flash'
Acer palmatum 'Red Pygmy'
Acer palmatum 'Red Spider'
Acer palmatum 'Red Spray'
Acer palmatum 'Red Upright'

Acer palmatum 'Red Wood'
Acer palmatum 'Roscoe Red'
Acer palmatum 'Royale'
Acer palmatum 'Ruby Lace'
Acer palmatum 'Ruby Ridge'
Acer palmatum 'Ruby Star'
Acer palmatum 'Rufescens'
Acer palmatum 'Rugose'
Acer palmatum 'Ryuzu'

Acer palmatum 'Sagara nishiki'
Acer palmatum 'Samidare'
Acer palmatum 'Sango kaku'
Acer palmatum 'Sanguineum'
Acer palmatum 'Sao shika'
Acer palmatum 'Saotome'
Acer palmatum 'Satzuki beni'
Acer palmatum 'Sazanami'
Acer palmatum 'Scolopendrifolium'
Acer palmatum 'Scolopendrifolium Rubrum'
Acer palmatum 'Seigai'
Acer palmatum 'Seigen'
Acer palmatum 'Seiryu'
Acer palmatum 'Sekimori'
Acer palmatum 'Sekka
Acer palmatum 'Sekka yatsubusa'
Acer palmatum 'Sentinel'
Acer palmatum 'Sessifolium'
Acer palmatum 'Shaina'
Acer palmatum 'Sharp's Pygmy'
Acer palmatum 'Sherwood Flame'
Acer palmatum 'Shidava Gold'
Acer palmatum 'Shigarami'
Acer palmatum 'Shigitatsu sawa'
Acer palmatum 'Shigure bato'
Acer palmatum 'Shigurezome'
Acer palmatum 'Shikageori nishiki'
Acer palmatum 'Shindeshojo'
Acer palmatum 'Shinobuga oka'
Acer palmatum 'Shinonomi'
Acer palmatum 'Shira Red'
Acer palmatum 'Shiranami'
Acer palmatum 'Shishi yatsubusa'

Acer palmatum 'Shishigashira'
Acer palmatum 'Shishio hime'
Acer palmatum 'Shishio Improved'
Acer palmatum 'Shojo
Acer palmatum 'Shojo nomura '
Acer palmatum 'Shojo shidare'
Acer palmatum 'Shuzanko'
Acer palmatum 'Sketer's Broom'
Acer palmatum 'Sode nishiki'
Acer palmatum 'Sode no uchi'

Acer palmatum 'Spring Delight'
Acer palmatum 'Stella Rossa'
Acer palmatum 'Suisei'
Acer palmatum 'Sumi nagashi'
Acer palmatum 'Sunglow'
Acer palmatum 'Sunny Sister'
Acer palmatum 'Sunset'
Acer palmatum 'Superbum'

Acer palmatum 'Taimin nishiki'
Acer palmatum 'Taiyo nishiki'
Acer palmatum 'Takao'
Acer palmatum 'Takinogawa'
Acer palmatum 'Tamahime'
Acer palmatum 'Tamukeyama
Acer palmatum 'Tana'
Acer palmatum 'Tanabata'
Acer palmatum 'Taroyama'
Acer palmatum 'Tatsuga nishiki'
Acer palmatum 'Tennyo no hoshi'
Acer palmatum 'The Bishop'
Acer palmatum 'Tiger Rose'
Acer palmatum 'Tiny Leaf'
Acer palmatum 'Tiny Tim'
Acer palmatum 'Tobiosho'
Acer palmatum 'Tokado'
Acer palmatum 'Toyama nishiki'
Acer palmatum 'Trompenburg'
Acer palmatum 'Tsuchigumo'
Acer palmatum 'Tsukushigata'
Acer palmatum 'Tsuma beni'
Acer palmatum 'Tsuma gaki'
Acer palmatum 'Tsuri nishiki'

Acer palmatum 'Ueno homare'
Acer palmatum 'Ueno yama'
Acer palmatum 'Ukigumo'
Acer palmatum 'Ukon'
Acer palmatum 'Umegae'
Acer palmatum 'Uncle Red'
Acer palmatum 'Us Murasaki'
Acer palmatum 'Utsu semi'
Acer palmatum 'Van der Akker'
Acer palmatum 'Variegatum'
Acer palmatum 'Ven's Broom'
Acer palmatum 'Ven's Red'
Acer palmatum 'Versicolor'
Acer palmatum 'Vic's Pink'
Acer palmatum 'Vic's Broom'
Acer palmatum 'Villa Taranto'
Acer palmatum 'Viridis'
Acer palmatum 'Vitifolium'
Acer palmatum 'Volubile'

Acer palmatum 'Wabito'
Acer palmatum 'Waka midori'
Acer palmatum 'Waka momiji'
Acer palmatum 'Waka momiji Variegated'
Acer palmatum 'Wakenhurst Pink'
Acer palmatum 'Walley's #1'
Acer palmatum 'Walley's #2'
Acer palmatum 'Walley's #3'
Acer palmatum 'Washi no o'
Acer palmatum 'Waterfall'
Acer palmatum 'Watnag'
Acer palmatum 'Wattez'
Acer palmatum 'Werner's Little Leaf'
Acer palmatum 'Werner's Pagoda'
Acer palmatum 'Wetumpka Red'
Acer palmatum 'Whitney Red'
Acer palmatum 'Will D'
Acer palmatum 'Willow Leaf'
Acer palmatum 'Will's Divine'
Acer palmatum 'Wilson Pink'
Acer palmatum 'Winter Flame'
Acer palmatum 'Wood Seedling'
Acer palmatum 'Wou nishiki'

Acer palmatum 'Yama hime'
Acer palmatum 'Yasemin'
Acer palmatum 'Yashio'
Acer palmatum 'Yellow Variegated'
Acer palmatum 'Yubae'
Acer palmatum 'Yugure'
Acer palmatum 'Yuri hime'

Maple Sources

Buchholz & Buchholz Nursery (W)
(503) 985-3253
Don Schmidt Nursery, Inc. (W)
(503) 668-4659
Firma C. Esveld
www.esveld.nl
Garden Kinosato
www.kinosato.net
Greer Gardens
www.greergardens.com
Iseli Nursery (W)
www.iseli-nursery.com
Kairyoen Co., Ltd.
www.kairyoen.co.jp
Maillot Bonsai
www.maillot-erable.com
Mountain Maples
www.mountainmaples.com
Nakajima Plantation Co., Ltd.
www.nnweb.co.jp
Sato Nursery
Tel: 048-296-7970
Shibamichi Honten
Tel: 048-296-3506
Stanley and Sons Nursery (W)
www.stanleyandsons.com
Tsukasa Engei
www5d.biglobe.ne.jp/~t-maple

Facing page foreground: *Sasa veitchii*
Behind wall: *Euonymus alatus*